THE FUTURE OF ELECTRIC VEHICLES

A SUSTAINABLE SOLUTION

TAIWO AYODELE

NEXTELECTRICCARS PUBLICATION TEAM

Website: **www.nextelectriccars.com**

Email Author: **author@nextelectriccars.com**

Twitter: **www.twitter.com/nextelectricar**

Tumblr: **www.nextelectriccars.tumblr.com**

Pinterest: **www.pinterest.co.uk/nextelectriccars**

Facebook: **www.facebook.com/nextelectriccars**

Instagram: **www.instagram.com/nextelectriccars**

Email Publication Team: **publicationteam@nextelectriccars.com**

Table of Contents

CHAPTER ONE

Brief History of Electric Vehicles

Electric vehicles (EV) or electric cars are seen as the future of transport because of their advanced power train technologies that primarily include a power source coupled with one or more electric motors to generate power. One thing that clearly distinguishes electric vehicles from conventional combustion vehicles is the fact that they produce zero emissions, and this makes them environmentally friendly.

Although the history of electric vehicles dates back to the early 19th century and electric power train technology is not new, the transition to electric vehicles has only begun to develop since the beginning of the 21st century. Some critical breakthroughs have been made in this sector in recent years and the future of electric vehicles now looks more and more promising than ever before.

Early Electric car[1]

[1] https://www.electricvehiclesnews.com/History/historyearlyIII.htm

Evolution of Electric Vehicles

The evolution of electric vehicles has not been easy, as many technological barriers have made it difficult and tedious to move from conventional vehicles to electric vehicles. The invention of electric vehicles cannot be tied to a particular inventor or a specific country, as many scientists and automotive experts from different countries have played their role in the evolution of electric vehicles. Let's explore the evolution of electric vehicles over time and see how concrete actions and dedicated efforts have led to the creation of the modern electric vehicles.

1832-1899 - A slow but steady start

Automotive engineers and scientists recognised the need for an alternative fuel vehicle in the early 19th century, but the development of this vehicle did not occur until after 1830. Between 1832 and 1899, the evolution was slow; the focus had been on scientists and experts emphasising the development of a long-lasting electric battery for commercial use. The first substantial advance in this regard was made by a Scottish inventor, Robert Anderson, who invented the first raw electric carriage, powered by non-rechargeable primary cells.

In 1835, Thomas Davenport of America built the first small practical electric vehicle powered by a DC electric motor.

In 1859, a significant contribution by French scientists improved the capacity of batteries to be used in electric vehicles. Gaston Plante, a physicist, invented the rechargeable lead-acid storage battery, then in 1981, another French scientist, Camille Faure, improved the battery's ability to supply power. He also invented the lead-acid base battery, which was then used in automobiles.

Electric vehicles were a great success from 1890 to 1900. The technologies had improved, and the major car manufacturers started to invest heavily in electric cars. In 1891, the first successful electric car was introduced to the United States by William Morrison. After that, many other companies introduced their own electric vehicles and the Connecticut-based Pope Manufacturing Company began large-scale production in 1897.

In 1899, Thomas Edison began working to improve the efficiency and capabilities of the electric battery used in automobiles. His efforts significantly improved the operation of alkaline batteries used in commercial vehicles.

Thomas Edison Electric car[2].

1900-1960 - The electric car industry goes through a decline

While the early twentieth century proved productive for electric vehicles, sales rising sharply in the United States in the 1900s, the next few decades saw almost no growth: the disappearance of electric cars seemed inevitable. While the popularity of combustion vehicles increased with inventions designed to improve power train technologies.

The decline of electric cars could be attributed to the following factors at this time:

- Easy availability of cheap gasoline
- Higher cost of electric cars
- Better power of conventional combustion engine cars

[2] https://www.treehugger.com/cars/quote-of-the-day-the-more-things-change-1916-book-on-electric-cars.html

- Progress in the development of fuel-efficient combustion engines
- Poor mileage of electric cars

In 1908, mass production of Henry Ford's Model T significantly affected the growth of electric vehicles as the Model T was one of the most advanced gasoline vehicles of the day. With better power characteristics, improved mileage and impressive overall performance, the Model T quickly became popular in the automobile markets. The electric car industry almost disappeared until 1960.

1960-2000 - The demand for electric vehicles increases again

Gasoline shortages and soaring oil prices after the Arab oil embargo turned the conventional combustion-powered cars into a costly option. It was also the time when global auto companies were beginning to find ways to reduce air pollution from combustion-engine vehicles; electric vehicles were being considered as an environmentally friendly alternative to conventional vehicles. Many countries, particularly the United States, had invested heavily in this research and development of electric vehicles, and many important advances had been made in increasing the capacity of electric cars.

In 1971, NASA developed this first electric lunar rover, which became the first manned vehicle to be driven on the moon. This was a major advance in the evolution of electric vehicles.

In 1973, General Motors built a prototype that was revealed at the first symposium of the Environmental Protection Agency. Around the same time, the American Motor Company developed electric delivery Jeeps, and 350 Jeeps were sold to the US Postal Service as part of a test program.

The years from 1970 to 1990 were marked by steady progress in the electric car industry, with a focus on research and development to explore new growth opportunities. During this period, many car manufacturers began to develop electric versions of their existing combustion engine vehicles. General Motors (GM) produced EV1 and developed it from 1966 to 1999. The EV1 was considered the most efficient standard electric vehicle in the world, but production was halted in 1999 because of high production cost.

21st Century - A new Start for Electric Vehicles

The foundation for a new start for electric cars had already been laid in the 20th century thanks to extensive research and the growing acceptance of vehicles such as the EV1 and other electric vehicles of this era. In the late 1990s, Toyota made a major breakthrough in alternative fuel vehicle production and launched its first hybrid vehicle, the Toyota Prius. It proved to be a hit with car enthusiasts and ushered in a new era for hybrid and electric vehicles that would promise improved driving range and advanced electric battery technologies.

The Toyota Prius used a nickel-metal hybrid battery, which improved vehicle efficiency and increased the popularity of alternative fuel vehicles around the world. Figure 1 shows the increase in popularity of the battery electric vehicle (BEV).

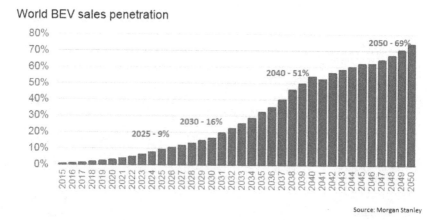

Figure 1: Increase in popularity of electric vehicles

After the success of the Toyota Prius, other car companies started producing electric vehicles on a large-scale vehicle and many new electric vehicles appeared on the market, including Honda EV Plus, Ford Ranger Pickup EV, Kia e-Niro, Hyundai Kona Electric, Nissan Altra EV, Toyota RAV4 EV, BMW i3 and the Chevrolet S-10 EV. Another major development that has transformed the future of electric vehicles was the announcement of a luxury electric sports car with an expected capacity of 383 kilometers and more or from 238 miles to 348 miles on a single charge from Tesla Motors. Since then, Tesla has continued to produce state-of-the-art electric vehicles and has been widely acclaimed for the production of excellent electric vehicles, including Tesla Model S, Tesla Model 3 and Tesla Model X and Tesla Model Y.

CHAPTER TWO

Why Electric Cars? The Case for Electric Vehicles

It is stated according to the World Health Organization's research that (WHO, 2019):

> Ambient air pollution accounts for an estimated 4.2 million deaths per year due to stroke, heart disease, lung cancer and chronic respiratory diseases. Around 91% of the world's population lives in places where air quality levels exceed WHO limits. While ambient air pollution affects developed and developing countries alike, low- and middle-income countries experience the highest burden, with the greatest toll in the WHO Western Pacific and South-East Asia regions. Policies and investments supporting cleaner transport, energy-efficient housing, power generation, industry and better municipal waste management can effectively reduce key sources of ambient air pollution.

In the wake of understanding the effects of pollution in the United Kingdom (UK), Michelle Roberts, BBC Health Editor, wrote (BBC News Online, 2016):

UK air pollution is linked to over 40,000 early deaths a year. Outdoor air pollution is contributing to about 40,000 early deaths a year in the UK, say the Royal Colleges of Physicians and of Pediatrics and Child Health. They say diesel emissions have been poorly controlled. And indoor air pollution has been overlooked. Tobacco still poses the biggest indoor threat, but wood-burning stoves, cleaning products and air fresheners can contribute. Mould and mildew in poorly ventilated rooms can also cause illness.

The World Health Organization report further elaborated (WHO, 2019):

Ambient (outdoor air pollution) is a major cause of death and disease globally. The health effects range from increased hospital admissions and emergency room visits, to increased risk of premature death. Worldwide ambient air pollution accounts for:

- 29% of all deaths and disease from lung cancer

- 17% of all deaths and disease from acute lower respiratory infection

- 24% of all deaths from stroke

- 25% of all deaths and disease from ischaemic heart disease

- 43% of all deaths and disease from chronic obstructive pulmonary disease

Human activities that are major sources of outdoor air pollution, include:

- Fuel combustion from motor vehicles (e.g. cars and heavy-duty vehicles)
- Heat and power generation (e.g. oil and coal power plants and boilers)
- Industrial facilities (e.g. manufacturing factories, mines, and oil refineries)
- Municipal and agricultural waste sites and waste incineration/burning
- Residential cooking, heating, and lighting with polluting fuels.

Poor urban planning, which leads to urban sprawl and over-dependence on private vehicle transport, is also a major factor in accelerated pollution emissions. Adverse health consequences to air pollution can occur as a result of short- or long-term exposure[3].

---

[3] https://www.who.int/airpollution/ambient/en/

It is also understood that the UK government is worried about the mortality rate due to air pollution as, "Electric vehicles (EVs) represent exciting opportunities for the UK: as a technology to reduce greenhouse gas emissions from the largest-emitting sector; as a tool to reduce local air pollution, the second-highest cause of avoidable mortality in the country" (House of Commons: HC 383, 2018).

The government's plan is to phase out sales of petrol and diesel cars and vans by 2040. It requires all new cars and vans to be effectively zero emission by 2050. Table 1 shows various governments' plans to end the sales of conventional vehicles.

Table 1: End Usage dates for Petrol & Diesel Cars or Vans

Countries	Timing
Norway	2025
India, China, Slovenia, Austria, Israel, the Netherlands, Ireland	2030
Scotland	2032
UK, France, Sri Lanka, Taiwan	2040

The transition to EV is set to increase over the coming years. Electric cars are becoming increasingly more popular in Europe, Asia, and US. The countries that are leading the way in promoting electric vehicles and detailing some underlying successful outcomes are elaborated in the International Council for Clean Transportation (ICCT) White Paper Report[1]:

'This report assesses major cities that are leaders in promoting electric vehicles around the world, quantifies their market successes to date, and discusses the underlying contributing factors for each. We identify 14 major metropolitan areas in North America, Europe, and China that led their respective countries in electric vehicle uptake or sales shares in 2015. Only metropolitan areas with a population over 1 million residents are included in this analysis.

For each city, we summarize the policy, infrastructure, and consumer awareness actions that have been put in place to grow the market in these world-leading electric vehicle markets.

The markets are evaluated at the metropolitan area level to incorporate the urban centre and the surrounding commuting area. We compare electric and conventional vehicle life-cycle emission data to assess the new technology's relative climatic impact in these pioneering electric vehicle markets.' (Hall et al., 2017).

Figure 2 illustrates electric vehicle sales and sales shares of the 14 electric vehicle capital cities from the report mentioned above. These are the foremost major markets in terms of their relatively rapid deployment of electric vehicles at the early stage of electric vehicle market growth in 2015.

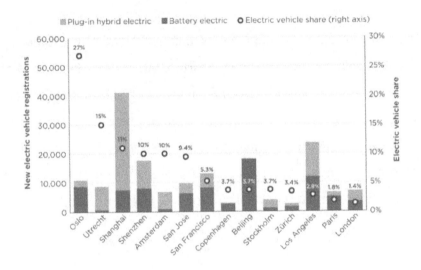

Figure 2: Electric vehicle new registrations and share of new vehicles in 2015 in high electric vehicle uptake markets (New vehicle registration data from IHS Markit and IHS Automotive)[4]

---

[4] theicct.org/sites/default/files/publications/Global-EV-Capitals_White-Paper_06032017_vF.pdf

Also, the ICCT White Paper explains that availability of charging infrastructures, governments' financial incentives, EVs' efficiency and the overall big savings on maintenance and running cost are key to consumers' recent interest in EVs. Furthermore, the ICCT White Paper[5] explicitly re-iterates the increase of consumers' interest in EVs (Hall et al., 2017):

> The availability of charging infrastructure is linked to electric vehicle uptake around the world. Greater charging availability helps address key consumer barriers regarding the range and the convenience of electric vehicles. Charging of vehicle batteries tends to be largely done at home, and several studies have shown that availability of home charging infrastructure can increase interest in electric vehicles.

Figure 3 shows savings on EVs over existing combustion engine vehicles. Electric cars offer the biggest savings over diesel in Norway (27%) as the battery-powered vehicles are exempt from a heavy registration tax as illustrated in Figure 3.

---

[5] theicct.org/sites/default/files/publications/Global-EV-Capitals_White-Paper_06032017_vF.pdf

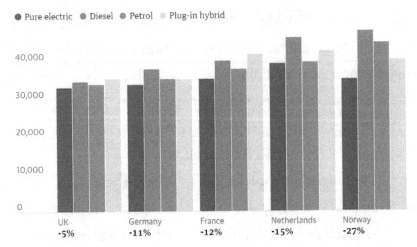

Figure 3: EVs Savings over Combustion Vehicles[2]

The UK's introduces incentives for the purchase of EVs. Figure 3 indicates that British drivers see the smallest savings of 5%. In Germany, France and the Netherlands, the savings varied from 11% to 15%.

CHAPTER THREE

How the Electric Car Works?

At last people are interested in electric cars and the benefits they offer: lower running costs, far less noise than petrol or diesel-engine rivals and lower car tax too. And if you buy one right now, you will also get up to £3500 off the price of a new car thanks to the government's plug-in vehicle grant in the UK. However, since November 2018 the grant has been available only for fully electric cars, not plug-in hybrid vehicles.

The batteries are most commonly positioned low in the car, and in some cases run along the floor. This helps to keep the car's center of gravity low, for stability when you around corners.

The battery stacks are heavy, though, which is why most electric cars weigh far more than conventional cars. The Renault Zoe, for example, weighs 1943kg, while the Ford Fiesta clocks in at 1620kg.

All electric vehicles (EVs) have an electric motor instead of an internal combustion engine. The vehicle uses a large traction battery pack to power the electric motor and must be plugged into a charging station or wall outlet to charge. Because it runs on electricity, the vehicle emits no exhaust from a tailpipe and does not contain the typical liquid fuel components, such as a fuel pump, fuel line, or fuel tank (AFDC, 2019).

Electric cars also commonly have an auxiliary battery to power the car's electrical systems, meaning the car's lights and infotainment system will still work if you run out of power from the main battery stack.

The electric motor is used to drive the car's wheels and, if two motors are used with one being placed on each axle, then electric cars can have four-wheel drive too. The Jaguar I-Pace, for example, has two electric motors and four-wheel drive, while the Nissan Leaf features one electric motor and is front-wheel drive.

Charging

Most fully electric cars and plug-in hybrids must be plugged in to recharge, either from a standard domestic socket, from a wall-mounted charger, or from a fast charger that you'll most commonly see at motorway service stations or in big towns and cities. In the future, you won't have to plug in an electric car to charge it: instead, you'll drive onto a special plate or space and the car will charge wirelessly, through a process known as inductive charging. Nissan, for example, has been working on inductive charging technology since 2009.

Fuel cell vehicles

Some electric cars get their electricity from a hydrogen fuel cell, and such cars are commonly referred to as fuel cell vehicles. There are many different types of hydrogen fuel cells at the moment, but most work on the same principle of combining hydrogen and oxygen to produce electricity and water. The Toyota Mirai and Hyundai Nexo are two examples of hydrogen fuel cell vehicles. Fuel cell vehicles must be filled with hydrogen from special filling stations, of which there are just 14 in the UK.

Control unit

Electric cars also feature a control unit, which is used to decide how much power from the batteries to send to the electric motor. If the controller functioned like a light switch and was only ever on or off, it would be nearly impossible to maintain speed. Instead, the controller drip-feeds power to the electric motor thousands of times every second, depending on the position of the accelerator, to emulate the feeling of driving a normal car. Despite this, electric cars generally accelerate very well, and this is because all of the car's torque – or pulling power – is available as soon as you put your foot down.

Regenerative braking

Electric cars can recuperate some of the energy normally lost in braking, and feed it back into the main battery to increase the range. In practice, this gives the sensation of the car slowing down as soon as you lift your foot off the accelerator.

Most electric cars let you customize how pronounced this effect is, but in some cases – for example, in the Nissan Leaf – you can effectively drive the car using just one pedal. Figure 4 shows components of all-electric vehicles.

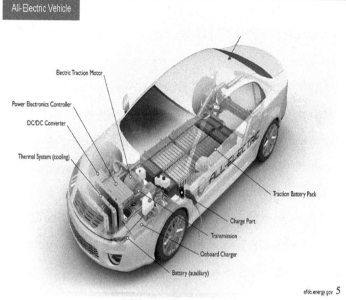

All-Electric Vehicle

Electric Traction Motor
Power Electronics Controller
DC/DC Converter
Thermal System (cooling)

Traction Battery Pack
Charge Port
Transmission
Onboard Charger
Battery (auxiliary)

afdc.energy.gov 5

Figure 4: Components of an electric car[6]

Key Components of an All-Electric Car

How all-electric cars work is elaborated in details by Energy Efficiency and Renewable Energy (EERE), alternative fuels data centre's research (AFDC, 2019):

Key components of an all-electric car

Battery (all-electric auxiliary): In an electric-powered vehicle, the auxiliary battery supplies electricity to power the vehicle's accessories.

---

[6] https://afdc.energy.gov/vehicles/how-do-all-electric-cars-work

Charging Port: The Charging Port allows the vehicle to connect to an external power source to charge the traction battery pack.

DC / AC converter: This unit converts the direct high-voltage current from the traction battery pack into a low-voltage DC battery needed to operate the vehicle accessories and recharge the auxiliary battery.

Electric Traction Motor: Powered by the traction battery pack, it drives the wheels of the vehicle. Some vehicles use generators that provide both drive and regeneration functions.

Onboard charger: Takes the alternative electricity provided by the charging port and converts it into a continuous power supply to charge the traction battery. It monitors battery characteristics such as voltage, current, temperature and state of charge while charging the pack.

Electronic Power Controller: This device manages the electrical energy flow provided by the traction battery, controlling the speed of the electric traction motor and the torque it produces.

Thermal System (Cooling): This system maintains an appropriate operating temperature range for the motor, electric motor, power electronics and other components.

Traction battery: Stores the electricity used by the electric traction motor.

Transmission (Electric): The transmission transfers the mechanical power of the electric traction motor to drive the wheels (AFDC, 2019).

CHAPTER FOUR

EV Charging Stations and Best EV Apps

There are government initiatives to help in reducing CO_2 emissions, mitigating climate change and improving air quality in Europe, North America, and Asia. As a result, there has been an increase of on-street EV charging stations in most cities which can be easily accessed by EV owners. You can easily charge your EV at home, in public charging stations, on-street parking places, supermarkets that have charging points, at workplace charging points, and etc.

It is now becoming easier to charge your EV on the go as there are more charging station infrastructures being built as the market for EVs keeps growing and more people are interested in EVs. Many drivers of electric vehicles are turning to their favorite apps or websites to plan their route or find a charger near their home. And you can also find the nearest charging points on a google map or EV Apps. Here are some of the most popular options.

Electric Vehicles Apps

PlugShare

https://www.plugshare.com/
Source: Google Play Store

PlugShare is a product of Recargo, based in El Segundo, California. PlugShare is "the flagship app for electric vehicle drivers" because it acts as a community for electric vehicle drivers, but it mostly guides users to public charging locations around the world. According to its website, the PlugShare application has been downloaded by 800,000 users.

Google Maps

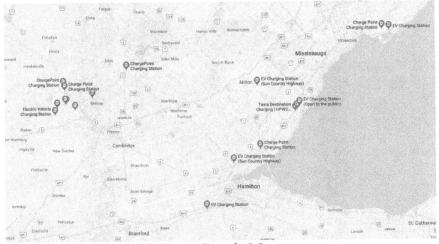

Source: Google Maps

In 2011, Google Maps added charging stations for electric vehicles to its list of features. A charging station is represented by a red GPS marker with a white charging station on it. The best part about using Google Maps to locate an electric vehicle charging station is that you are similarly using Street View so you can see exactly where the charging station is.

Open Charge Map

https://openchargemap.org/
Source: Google Play Store

Open Charge Map is a non-commercial, non-profit service hosted and supported by a community of businesses, charities, developers, and stakeholders from around the world. Their goal is to work with these stakeholders to develop and provide a high quality, free and open public database for charging electric cars locations around the world. As of April 2018, their map lists 121,874 charging stations in 61,178 locations.

ChargeHub

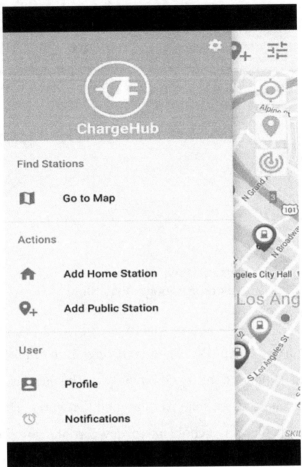

Source: chargehub.com
https://chargehub.com/en/

ChargeHub is known to be a dynamic community of more than 100,000 users and a dedicated team committed to improving the charging experience at public places.

Together they contribute to the development of a more user-friendly electric vehicle charging infrastructure in the United States and Canada. According to their website, users can find all the charging stations in Canada and the United States with their live update card.

ChargeMap

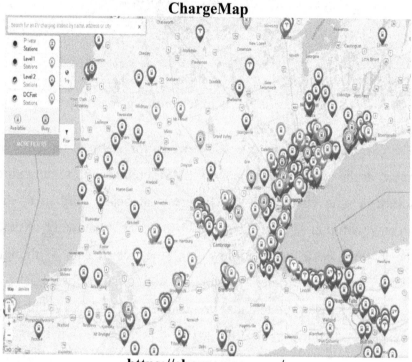

https://chargemap.com/
Source: Chargemap

Chargemap offers the largest map to find charging stations in Europe. Their mobile app allows drivers to add images, comments, charging stations and other useful information. Their map lists 55,733 charging locations with 181,384 stations and more than 160,000 members. The application is based in Europe but is listed worldwide.

EVSE Manufacturer of EV Charging Products

Source: https://www.evse.com/msgBoard.jsp

EVSE specializes in everyday needs for normal charging at home, at the office, or on the road. EVSE created smarter charging solutions with customers' best interests at heart. Plug in to the green revolution — right here, right now. This company created the charging cables compatible with all the electric cars. With high focus on safety, efficiency, mobility and great software EVSE wants you to use products that you can rely on and carry with you every day on your trips (EVSE, 2019).

Companies like FLO EV Charing network and ChargePoint also offer their own smart charging cards to their customers. The maps list not only their own charging stations, but also other options for electric vehicle drivers, so they are not stranded without a place to charge their battery. The electric vehicle manufacturer, Tesla, also offers a map showing its network of compressors.

FLO – EV Charging Network

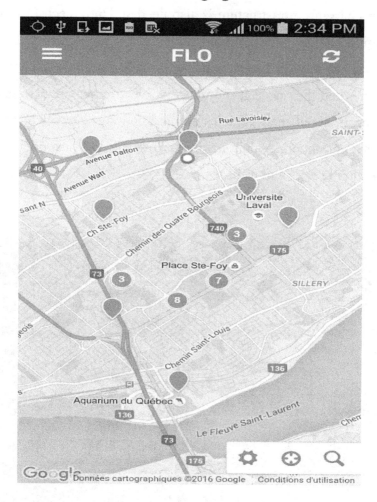

FLO – EV Charging
Source: Google Play Store

As electric vehicles continue to gain popularity, the demand for better-charging infrastructure is also needed. Until electric vehicle charging stations are as ubiquitous as gas stations, many drivers will have to rely on these great apps or websites to find a charging station when they need it. Fortunately, electric vehicle drivers are passionate about their vehicles and are coming together to create healthy communities that help improve the user experience of these mobile apps and websites.

ZAP MAP

Source: **https://www.zap-map.com/app/**

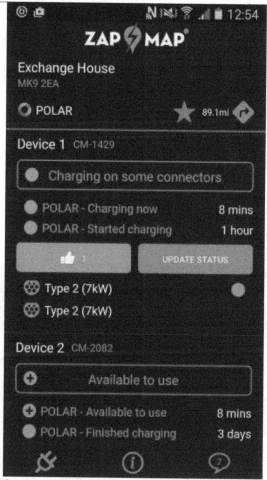

Source: **https://www.zap-map.com/app/**

UK-wide   charging   point   map

The Zap-Map electric car charging app offers a UK-wide charging point map currently showing over 6,000 charging locations and over 19,000 connectors. Clicking the zap-map menu gives users the option to search UK charge points, filter chargers or plan a route. In addition to the map view, there is also a list view, accessible from the navigation bar.

Use filters to identify suitable charge points

Zap-Map App users can filter map results by any combination of charge point type (slow, fast, rapid AC and rapid DC), connectors, location type, payment and access type.

How can I find EV chargers in Europe?

In Europe, finding EV Charging points is now very easy, especially with the help of Maps and EV Apps such as PlugShare. PlugShare is one of the most well-known and accurate public charging maps worldwide with stations from most major networks in Europe and in North America.

And there are several other big networks of charging stations in Europe such as **Chargemap and this App will display**[7]:

- Where charge points are located

- What type of connectors they have (you can filter results by connector or car type), including Tesla connectors

- Charge speed

- How to pay

- Whether the charger is being used or out of order

---

[7] https://www.theaa.com/european-breakdown-cover/driving-in-europe/charging-around-europe-in-an-electric-vehicle

Resources such as this provide an opportunity for users to provide information about their visits such as precise location ('behind the building, on the left'), nearby facilities, whether there are any issues or problems and to upload photographs.

Like in the UK, chargers are generally found where cars are likely to be parked for a while:

- Car parks

- On-street parking

- Shopping centres

- Restaurants

- Hotels

- Tourist attractions

You are increasingly likely to find fast chargers at conventional fuel stations and, of course, at most motorway service areas[5].

CHAPTER FIVE

Public EV Chargers

For drivers of electric vehicles who want to charge them regularly in public, it is important to know the charging networks that provide access to electric fuel when you travel. Each network works a little differently. It is a good idea for EV owners to have a basic understanding of how they compare to each other.

Cost Considerations

The three main approaches are[6]:

    (1) Pay-as-you-go

    (2) Pay Monthly

    (3) Free subscriptions and Free Charging Points

    (in some Super-markets)

Obviously, if given the opportunity, it is wise to take advantage of charging for free options, even for a relatively short period. But compensation models, based on the cost of fees, need to be studied to determine which network is best for you. You can decide whether it is better to collect a wallet filled with membership cards; or if proper planning will allow you to avoid public stations unless your battery is at a very low charge.

There are some pitfalls

Remember that the distance you can travel per hour depends on the power capabilities of your car's onboard charger. As Marc Geller, a director at Plug In America, an EV advocacy organization, told us: *"If the car comes with a smaller charger, the cost is relatively higher than if you have a faster charger"*. Other factors include credit card transactions and the costs of leaving the car plugged in, even if the battery is fully charged and the electrons have stopped flowing. To avoid these pitfalls, some networks have an unlimited charging plan[8].

As of March 2018, the majority of public chargers are still available for free in US and in the UK most of the charging points especially the ones located in most super-markets are still free.

EV Charging: How to prepare

Recharging your car can seem daunting, especially when there are many factors involved.

Here are some ways to avoid common mistakes:

---

[8] https://www.plugincars.com/ultimate-guide-electric-car-charging-networks-126530.html

Know the incentives before buying

This advice applies to purchase incentives and billing incentives. Knowing your final price (after incentives) will make your decision easier. Factor in reducing fuel and maintenance costs as well as in the cost of ownership over the next few years.

Make sure your home electrical system is ready. Amperage is important when installing a charging station, so make sure that the area in which you plan to install the station can support 30 amps. Check with the electricians in your area to find out how much the installation will cost.

Find stations near your workplace and other regular stops. Knowing that you have charging options near your job, your favorite park or another regular stop will allow you to get level 2 energy quickly while you do your errands.

Know where the free chargers are

In addition to the many public pay stations, many free options are available. Find out where they are in your area and take advantage of them when necessary. In some cases, dealers selling your electric vehicle model allow customers to charge for free. In the UK, most supermarkets such as Tesco, Sainsbury's, ASDA, Morrisons provide free (at least for now) charging points for electric cars. A standard 7kW charger will be available for free, but electric car owners will have to pay for a faster service. You can also use PlugShare App to find free EV charging stations near you. It covers all EVs connected communities in the world.

Note the locations of convenient quick chargers

Having a fast charger near you will be useful if you need a complete battery charge on demand. Before subscribing to a charge provider package, you need to get an idea of how you can activate it quickly. Look for savings outside of peak hours. Peak electricity costs can be up to three times the cost during off-peak periods. Find out if your utility provider offers programs for electric vehicle drivers to find the lowest rates.

Currently, there are three main types of EV charging; rapid charging, fast charging, and slow charging with various type of connections that represent the power outputs and charging speeds that are available to charge EVs.

This charging power is measured in kilowatts (kW). Here are examples of EV Charging connector types[9]:

1. Rapid Chargers

These are the type of chargers that are often found in motorway services and as the name implies, these are the fastest type of chargers, and comes in both AC and DC forms with:

- 43kW AC charging on one connector type

- 50kW DC charging on one of two connector types

- 120kW DC charging on Tesla Supercharger network

- All rapid units have fastened and connected cables

Here are EV Chargers Examples:

CHAdeMO: 50 kW DC

[9] https://www.zap-map.com/charge-points/connectors-speeds/

CCS: 50 kW DC

The EV can be recharge in DC or AC to 80% in 20-40 minutes. Generally, the charging units power down when the battery is about 80% full to protect the battery in order to extend its life. All rapid devices have the charging cable fastened to the unit. Rapid AC chargers will use a Type 2 connector, while Rapid DC connectors use CCS or the CHAdeMO standard.

2. Fast Chargers

Fast chargers are ideal for home use and they are one of the most common types of chargers. All faster chargers are AC type, they are either 7 kW or 22 kW (Single or three-phase 32A).

- 7kW fast charging on one of three connector types

- 11kW fast charging on Tesla charging station

- 22kW fast charging on one of three connector types

Type 2: 43 kW AC

Telsa Type: 120 kW DC

Type 2: 7 -11 kW AC

Charging times vary on unit speed and the vehicle, but a 7 kW charger will recharge a compatible EV with a 30-kWh battery in 3-5 hours, and a 22-kW charger in 1-2 hours. While for a 7 kW charger will recharge a compatible EV with a 64-KWh battery in 8-10 hours.

Fast chargers tend to be found at places, such as workplace car parks, super-markets, public car parks, or leisure centres where you are likely be parked at for an hour or for a longer period of time.

Type 1: 7 kW AC

3 – Pin: 3 kW AC

3. Slow Chargers

Slow charging is a very slow way of charging electric vehicles, and some EV owners use this method to charge their EV at home. The slow chargers have a three-pin plug using a standard 3-pin socket.

- 3kW slow charging on one of four connector types

- Includes mains charging and from specialist chargers

- Often covers home charging

Most slow charging units are 3 kW while some lamp post chargers on street parking could 6 kW. Charging times vary depending on the charging unit and EV being charged, but a full charge on a 3-kW unit will usually take between 6-12 hours. The charging time varies[10].

---

[10] https://pod-point.com/guides/driver/how-long-to-charge-an-electric-car

CHAPTER SIX

Smart Charging

What is smart charge?

To meet the high demand of the grid without the use of expensive and nonrenewable sources, many utility companies have introduced time-based pricing for commercial and residential customers. The idea is to charge higher rates during peak periods to encourage users to shift high-demand energy requirements during off-peak hours.

This goes even further in that it allows for variable power usage during peak and off-peak periods. Some pilot programmes have already started with EV owners who want to charge their vehicles at the lowest possible price. Using such a programme, a utility will slow down billing when the demand is high, then return to normal billing when the demand on the network clears.

As of March 2018, the majority of public chargers are still available for free (although not all systems know exactly how much electric vehicle drivers pay to charge). There are nearly 47,000 free public places to charge an EV, while there are not quite 40,000 paid public places. (These numbers do not include the nearly 2,000 paid sites that are not fully public, such as places where only employees of a company can charge).

Charging Station Infrastructure

Electric car charging stations are an exciting invention of the modern era. The transition away from traditional fuels, like gasoline, towards electricity, helps to reduce greenhouse gases, and carbon dioxide emissions, reducing the emissions of fossil fuels and is generally cheaper for the consumer in the long run.

List of EV Charging Networks

BLINK NETWORK

List of Top EV Charging Networks[11]

---

[11] https://www.plugincars.com/ultimate-guide-electric-car-charging-networks-126530.html

Access: Start by registering a credit card with a Blink account. There are no required annual or monthly membership fees, or minimum credit card balance.

Members who register will receive an "InCard" and can initiate a charge using the card. Guests can initiate a charge with Blink's mobile application.

Cost Per Charge: In the states that permit kilowatt-hour pricing, fees for Level 2 EV charging stations owned by Blink and operated on the Blink Network range from $0.39 to $0.79 per kWh, depending on the state and individual's membership status. Blink is a proponent of kWh pricing because it is usage-based and EV drivers pay fees based on the actual amount of power consumed during the charging session rather than the amount of time that the car is plugged into the station. Fees for DCFC chargers owned by Blink and operated on the Blink Network in kWh eligible states range from $0.49 to $0.69 per kWh, depending on the state and individual's membership status.

Website: http://www.blinknetwork.com

Technical Support: 24/7 technical support

POD POINT

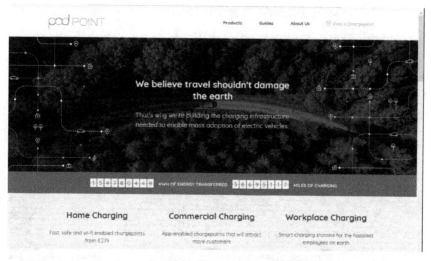

Source: **https://pod-point.com/**

PodPoint[12] provides a guide on how to charge electric car, places you can top up your battery and how to start charging once you are there in the UK. To charge an electric car, you will need to plug it into a charging point. In the UK there are four main places you can find these; at home, at work, at public locations and at service stations. You will sometimes need to take your own separate charging cable with you. Most EV drivers' plug-in to a chargepoint whenever they park to stay topped up.

---

[12] https://pod-point.com/guides/driver/how-to-charge-electric-car

Most supermarkets in the UK such as Tesco, Sainsbury's, ASDA, Morrisons provide free (at least for now) charging points for electric cars anytime on 7 kW charger. While Lidl allows 90mins max EV charging on different types of chargers including rapid charger (50 kW). The idea is that customers will be able to charge their EVs while shopping.

CHARGEPOINT

Access: There is no cost to sign up and receive a ChargePoint card. After submitting your credit card information as part of the sign-up, you will be charged an initial deposit of $25 only when you first visit a charging station that requires a fee (Many stations on the network are free). Your account provides access to all public stations on ChargePoint. Charging stations are activated with the ChargePoint card or a contactless credit card. The stations can also be activated by calling a toll-free customer service number on the ChargePoint station, or by using the associated mobile app. Account balances automatically replenish when the balance gets low.

Cost per Charge: Prices are determined by the property owner. Many ChargePoint stations are free.

Website: http://www.chargepoint.com

Technical Support: 24/7 customer support

THE ELECTRIC CIRCUIT

Access: There is no cost to sign up and receive an Electric Circuit card. When you first order your Electric Circuit card, you will be charged $10 (tax included), which will give you four charging sessions at any 240-V station or a 1-hour charge at any fast charge station. You will then be able to add money to your account as you wish.

Cost per charge: The rate for a 240-V charge is a flat fee of $2.50 (tax included), no matter how long you use the charging station. As of October 1st, 2014, fast-charging is offered at $10 per hour and billed by the minute. This rate applies to all existing and future fast-charge stations of the Electric Circuit.
Website: http://www.lecircuitelectrique.com/index.en.html

Tech Support: Electric Circuit users have access to a 24/7 telephone helpline. The Electric Circuit Web site, theelectriccircuit.com, and the mobile application for iOS and Android are updated as new stations are installed or commissioned.

EVGO

Source: evgonetwork.com

EVgo is one of the largest public fast charging networks for electric vehicles. It provides the best driver experience and station reliability in the industry. EVgo stations offer the fastest speeds available in public charging – up to 8 times faster than other networks.

Source: evgo.com

Access: NRG's network is only available to its monthly subscribers using an EVgo card, but as its website states, the company "will always take care of an EV driver in need of a charge."

Cost per Charge: There are no setup, termination, or session fees. All Level 2 charging is $1.50 per hour. For DC Quick Charging, the pay-as-you-go plan costs $0.20/minute.

If you are a member at $9.99 per month, the cost drops to $0.15/minute. The length of time for a charge depends on the time of day according to EVgo[26].

Website: http://www.evgo.com/

Technical Support: Contact support@evgo.com.

GREENLOTS

Access: Users have many access options, including (1) Downloading the free Greenlots app from iTunes or Google Play. Next, enter your credit card information. Once your information is saved, select "Charge" from the menu and enter the Station ID or scan the QR code displayed on the front of the station; (2) Swipe your Greenlots RFID card; (3) Call the customer care number listed on the station to have the charge session started remotely; and (4) Some stations have a credit card swiper. Users can also create a driver account at www.charge.greenlots.com to track electricity usage, update information, or order a RFID card.

Coverage: No specific region. Charging stations in Midwest, Northeast, Northwest, South, and Southwest, as well as Hawaii, Canada and Singapore. Cost Per Charge: Site hosts determine the fee for use. Greenlots does not charge a membership fee.

Website: http://greenlots.com/

Technical Support: 24/7/365 customer care. Less urgent inquiries can be sent to support@greenlots.com.

SEMACONNECT

Access: To sign up, log on to the SemaConnect website, and open a new account. You will receive a RFID card that can be used to initiate charging at any SemaConnect location. A SemaConnect account is free, however, if you choose to set up an autopay feature with your account, your credit or debit card will be charged an initial $10.00. This money is not a charge by SemaConnect, but rather it is what turns your SemaConnect account into a debit system for charging your electric vehicle and will be utilized to pay for your charging sessions with money being deducted based on the pricing structure of your charging location.

When your initial $10.00 is depleted, your associated card will automatically be charged $20.00 to replenish your account. $20.00 is the minimum replenishment amount, but you can choose to replenish your card with up to $250.00.

Cost per charge: The cost varies, as determined by the property owner.

Website: http://www.semaconnect.com

Tech support: Available 9 am to 5 pm

TESLA SUPERCHARGERS and TESLA DESTINATION CHARGERS

Access: Tesla Superchargers do not require a card to initiate access. Tesla owners can simply drive up and plug in.

Cost Per Charge: As of January 1, 2017, anyone who orders a Tesla will get 400 kWh of free Supercharging credits per year, good for about 1,000 miles of driving.

Tesla has not revealed how much it will cost after that limit but says a "small fee" that will be cheaper than buying gas. Owners who ordered their car in 2016 or earlier will still charge for free, for life. That excludes owners of the Tesla Model 3.

Website: http://www.teslamotors.com/supercharger

Technical Support: Available toll-free

WEBASTO EV SOLUTIONS (FORMERLY AEROVIRONMENT)

Access: Unlimited monthly access is provided for $19.99 per month. Subscribing to the Webasto network starts by calling 888-833-2148 or filling out a form on the Webasto's website.

The company will send a key fob that activates the chargers. If you are a current subscriber there is no activation fee. If you are a new subscriber, there will be a one-time activation fee of $15.

Cost per charge: As an alternative to the flat monthly access fee, there is the option of paying per session: $7.50/session for DC Fast Charger; and $4.00/session for a Level 2 charging station (Per session payment is only available by calling the Customer Service Support Line at 888-833-2148).

Website: https://www.evsolutions.com/ev-network

Tech Support: 24/7 support. AV can also be emailed at info.us@webasto-charging.com

INSTALLING THE EV CHARGING STATIONS

Before going into details on different aspects of the load, let's define some key terms:

Onboard charger: The charger used for Level 1 and Level 2 recharges is installed at the factory and is called an "on-board charger." It converts the alternating current of the wall into a direct current that charges the battery in the vehicle.

Charging speed may vary, but the most common on-board chargers are 6.6 kW on battery electric vehicles (BEV) and 3.3 kW on plug-in hybrid electric vehicles (PHEV). The DC fast charge uses its own external charger.

EVSE: means "electric vehicle service equipment". It is an intermediate between a power source and the vehicle charging port. It is usually mounted on a wall or pedestal. Its role is merely to relay the AC power to the vehicle safely.

Level 1 Charging: The slowest form of charging. Uses a plug to connect to the built-in charger and a standard 120V household outlet. This configuration provides between 2 and 5 miles per hour. Although it does not sound adequate at all, it can work for those who travel less than 40 km a day and have all night to recharge.

Level 2 Charging: Uses an EVSE to provide power at 220V or 240V and up to 30A. Drivers can add 10 to 25 km of range in one hour of charging at home or in a public station.

Fast DC Charging: Some companies talk about Level 3 charging. In this case, the charger is a machine the size of a gas pump. There is no single standard for fast charging - Tesla has the Supercharger network. The Nissan Leaf and other models make the best use of CHAdeMO, and another group uses SAE Combo. All of the above fast chargers provide approximately 80% charge in 30 minutes.

Electric Vehicle Service Provider (EVSP): An EVSP provides connectivity over a network of charging stations. By connecting to a central server, they manage the software, the database and the communication interfaces allowing the operation of the station.

CHAPTER SEVEN

Electric Vehicle Battery Types

A battery is a device that stores chemical energy and converts that chemical energy into electricity (figure 5).

Although there are many types of batteries, the basic concept for how they operate remains the same. When a device is connected to a battery, there is a reaction that produces electrical energy. This is known as an electrochemical reaction. The Italian physicist, Count Alessandro Volta, discovered this process in 1799 when he created a simple pile from metal plates and cardboard or paper soaked in brine. Since then, scientists have significantly improved Volta's original design to create batteries made of various materials, available in a multitude of sizes.

Figure 5: Lithium-ion (Li-ion)

Lithium-ion (Li-ion) batteries are now considered the norm for modern battery electric vehicles. There are many types of Li-ion batteries each with different characteristics, but the car manufacturers use concentrated variants offering excellent durability. Compared to other mature battery technologies, Li-ion offers many advantages. For example, it has great specific energy (140 Wh / kg) and energy density, making it ideal for battery electric vehicles.

Li-ion batteries also retain excellent energy, with a low self-discharge rate (5% per month) an order of magnitude lower than that of NiMH batteries. However, Li-ion batteries also have some disadvantages. Comparatively, Li-ion batteries are costly battery technology. Overcharging and overheating of these batteries also pose significant safety concerns. Li-ion often undergoes a thermal runaway, which can trigger vehicle fires or explosions. There were cases where the Tesla Model S, which used Li-ion batteries, caught fire infamously due to fluctuating charging problems or battery damage. However, great efforts have been made to improve the safety of vehicles using Li-ion batteries

Figure 6: Solar Panels

Electric and solar vehicles are often classified as green technologies, but what is their exact relationship? Should the solar industry pay attention to what happens with electric vehicles? It is important to look at all the potential technologies together because they are complementary. EVs can be charged during the day at the parking areas with full functioning solar panel systems as shown in figure 6. And the energy generated in each parking area is crucial for the extra generation of adequate electricity for transportation requirements for the EVs.

There is a lot of synergy between them, "EVs reduce battery costs simply by volume, and as more people drive electric vehicles, they will need a place to charge them, which will create even more potential for solar energy.

Solar Power Electric Car Charging Stations

Since the purpose of EVs is to reduce CO2 emissions, to mitigate climate change and to increase air quality, it is imperative that alternative and sustainable charging infrastructures are available as the market interest of EVs is growing. Luke John Smith (Smith, 2019) explained:

> A brand-new electric car charging station, which is one of over 100, is set to be built in Braintree, Essex. The UK-bound EV charging station is being built by Gridserve (Figure 7 and 8) and will have enough points to charge 24 cars at once. The stations will be placed along busy roads which will recharge hybrid and electric vehicles in half an hour. Electric cars with smaller batteries and high-speed charging capacities will also be able to recharge in just 10 minutes at these stations. If this is true and can be achieved, it will certainly make owning an electric car much easier (Figure 7).

Figure 7: Gridserve electric car charging station (Image: GRIDSERVE)

The plan is to eliminate EVs range anxiety as further expounded:

"We plan to eliminate any range or charging anxiety by building a UK-wide network of customer-focused, brand new Electric Forecourts that will make it easier and cheaper to use an electric vehicle than a petrol or diesel alternative. Within five years we plan to have more than 100 Electric Forecourts in use, with each on supported by solar energy and battery storage.

This infrastructure will accelerate the electric vehicle revolution, serve the grid, and help the UK meet climate and clean air targets.

We are partnering with operators of fleet vehicles, developers, financiers of vehicles and infrastructure, EV manufacturers, retailers, local authorities, and others who share our vision" (Smith, 2019).

Figure 8: Gridserve electric car charging station (Image: GRIDSERVE)

Hydrogen Battery

Hydrogen cars have been a polarising topic for years. At its core, a hydrogen car is an electric vehicle with a small onboard battery that is continuously charged by a hydrogen fuel cell that pulls in stored hydrogen gas, mixes it with oxygen from the atmosphere, and runs it through a proton exchange membrane, releasing electricity along the way. The only byproduct of this process is water, making the vehicle essentially just an electric vehicle that gets its power from a different type of onboard battery drivetrain according to CleanTechnica — the Toyota Mirai and the Honda Clarity Fuel Cell — and they both drive and operate like "normal" vehicles, which is great (See figure 9).

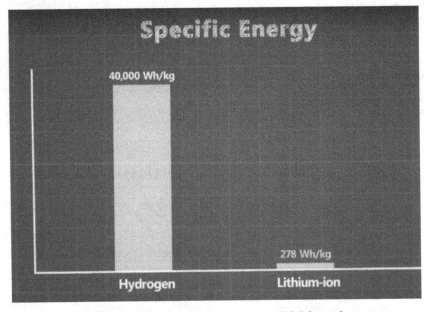

Figure 9: Hydrogen Battery vs Lithium-ion

The numbers behind hydrogen are compelling. Its specific energy — or the amount of energy it contains in a given weight — is far higher than that of lithium-ion batteries. One kilogram of hydrogen can store 236 times more energy than a kilogram of lithium-ion batteries (Figure 9).

Charging Electric Vehicles on the Go

Range anxiety is now a thing of the past especially now that there are several ways to charge an electric car such as; on-street parking points, supermarket charging points, home charging, city-wide charging stations, motorway fast charging stations, solar charging stations, and now wireless charging on the go as expounded by Tom Bawden (Bawden, 2019):

"Electric cars will be charged wirelessly while on the move in an initiative designed to revolutionise transport in the UK. Coventry intends to create the UK's first public 'E-lane' next year by installing wireless chargers on to a stretch of road in the north east of the city.

'Electric charging lanes have the potential to revolutionise the transport system' Cllr Jim O'Boyle, of Coventry City Council
It will, if successful, pave the way for electric vehicle use to become widespread across the UK and beyond within 10 years, experts say.

"Charging batteries on the move is key to the success of electric vehicles in the UK, not least because it will take away the anxiety many people feel about finding a charging station before it's too late," said project leader Shamala Evans, of Coventry City Council." Figure 10 illustrates further on the wireless charging lane.

E – Lane and Autonomous Vehicles

E-lanes will also smooth the way for driverless vehicles to become widespread, especially those designed to transport elderly, disabled or very young passengers who cannot drive and would find it difficult to locate and use a charging station (Figure 10).

An influx of vehicles on the road if autonomous vehicles do take off would put even more pressure on roadside charging stations, further increasing the need for on-the-road-charging facilities, according to Professor Mohammad Reza Mousavi, of the University of Leicester (Bawden, 2019).

"Autonomous vehicles could, for example, allow you to send your kid to school without being involved, so you can drive somewhere else. But you would need 'inductive charging' for them to become widely used.

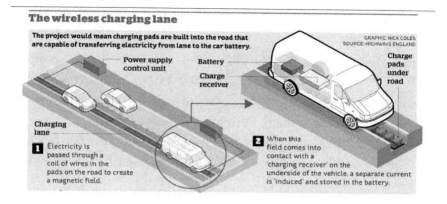

Figure 10: The wireless charging lane[13]

It is expected that many of the autonomous lorries of the future will be devoid of people altogether, making manual recharging even more difficult. But with electric lanes, these lorries could theoretically work around the clock. The world's first public road in the world that can wirelessly recharge electric-car batteries while they are on the move is due to open in the US state of Illinois early next year. Similar e-roads catering for buses and trucks are due to begin operations on the Swedish island of Gotland and in Tel Aviv, Israel around the same time[9]." While the funding for this project is still being finalised.

---

[13] https://inews.co.uk/news/science/electric-vehicles-charge-wireless-e-lanes-road-coventry/

Autonomous vehicles

It is expected that many of the autonomous lorries of the future will be devoid of people altogether, making manual recharging even more difficult. But with electric lanes, these lorries could theoretically work around the clock. Similar e-roads catering to buses and trucks are due to begin operations on the Swedish island of Gotland and in Tel Aviv, Israel around the same time (Bawden, 2019).

CHAPTER EIGHT

UK & US Government Incentives for Owning Electric Cars

Government provides some financial support towards purchasing electric vehicles

Government incentives for plug-in hybrid electric vehicles have been put in place by several national governments and local authorities around the world to support the adoption of the plug-in electric vehicle. These incentives are primarily purchase rebates, tax exemptions and tax credits, as well as additional benefits ranging from access to bus lanes to fee exemptions (parking, tolls, congestion charges etc.). The amount of financial incentives usually depends on the size of the battery and the total autonomy of the vehicle. Some countries are extending the benefits to fuel cell vehicles and conversions of hybrid electric vehicles and conventional internal combustion engine vehicles to electric vehicles.

The first mass-produced plug-in cars by major manufacturers began selling in late December 2010, with the launch of the all-electric Nissan Leaf and the Chevrolet Volt plug-in hybrid. Cumulative global sales of light-duty electric passenger cars and light commercial vehicles surpassed one million units in September 2015, reaching 4 million in September 2018, roughly one in 300 vehicles on the world's roads.

UK Car Grant Plug-in Offers Reduction on Low and No Emissions Vehicles

The UK rechargeable vehicle subsidy (PiCG) offered discounts on a selection of plug-in hybrid vehicles (PHEVs) and electric vehicles (Vs). However, the 2018 reforms ended financial support for PHEVs, while the maximum subsidy for electric vehicles was reduced from £ 4,500 to £3,500.

While in the US a similar scheme is in operation with a $7,500 tax credit. And in the UK, you will likely be exempt from Vehicle Excise Duty, Fuel Duty and company car tax. In London you do not have to pay the Congestion Charge and will often find that you can park in Pay and Display spaces for free. The grant provides a cash incentive that reduces the list price of electric vehicles currently on sale in the UK to encourage people to buy, with the aim of reducing emissions and improving air quality.

The system has been in place since 2011, although with the arrival of more and more alternative fuel vehicles, the government has adjusted the PiCG in 2016 and 2018 accordingly. If you bought an eligible car before 2016, the government paid £5,000 of the list price. In 2016, this amount was reduced, while PHEVs received a reduced grant. This means that purchasers of complete electric vehicles benefit from a maximum reduction of £4,500, while plug-in hybrid vehicle purchasers get £2,500 off their list price.

The 2018 amendments further reduced the total subsidy for electric vehicles to £3,500, while completely removing PHEVs from the system. The discount program, as well as the generous rates that benefit corporate car buyers, have resulted in an increase in the number of electric vehicles for sale, and the government has confirmed that the incentive will remain in place at least until 2020 - although in a reduced amount.

Which cars qualify for the PiCG?

If you want to buy an EV or plug-in hybrid, you'll want to know if the car you are buying is eligible for the PiCG, and the handy guide below will tell you the type of discount you can get. First, you need to know if your car belongs to one of the three categories of low-emission vehicles that the government supports to determine if a vehicle is eligible for the PiCG as follows:

- Category 1: vehicles with a range of 70 km producing zero emissions and a manufacturer with CO_2 emissions of less than 50 g / km.

- Category 2: vehicles with a range of at least 10 miles producing zero emissions, and a manufacturer that has reported CO_2 emission values of less than 50 g / km.

- Category 3: vehicles with an autonomy of at least 20 miles and emitting zero emissions, and a manufacturer citing CO_2 emissions between 50 and 75 g / km.

If your car qualifies for category 1, you can then enjoy the maximum PiCG, which pays 35% of the value of the car, for a maximum amount of £3,500.

Category 2 and 3 vehicles had a 35% discount if they cost less than £ 60,000, the maximum amount saved is £2,500. However, with the 2018 reforms, cars in categories 2 and 3 are no longer eligible for PiCG.

It should also be noted that only Category 1 vehicles are currently considered full electric vehicles, a plug-in all-in-one hybrid vehicle emitting less than 50g of CO_2 per kilometres and capable of traveling 70 kilometres on electrical power could technically qualify for the PiCG.

The purpose of these incentives is to encourage buyers to opt for the lowest emissions vehicles, in particular, full electric vehicles, rather than just encouraging buyers to switch to save on the original purchase value of their cars and then not use the hybrid element of the vehicle to help lower emissions when driving. Developing a zero-emission electric vehicle costs a whole lot more. So, they tend to have a higher purchase price than a similar vehicle running on gasoline, diesel or even a hybrid. This is why lower emitting cars always benefit from the maximum PiCG.

US Electric Vehicles Financial Incentives

While in the US, the federal government[14] and a number of states offer financial incentives, including tax credits, for lowering the up-front costs of plug-in electric vehicles (also known as electric cars or EVs). The federal Internal Revenue Service (IRS) tax credit is for $2,500 to $7,500 per new EV purchased for use in the U.S. The size of the tax credit depends on the size of the vehicle and its battery capacity. To find out specific tax credit amounts for individual vehicles, visit FuelEconomy.gov's Tax Credits for Electric Vehicles and Tax Credits for Plug-in Hybrids pages. This tax credit will be available until 200,000 qualified

---

[14] https://www.energy.gov/eere/electricvehicles/electric-vehicles-tax-credits-and-other-incentives

EVs have been sold in the United States by each manufacturer, at which point the credit begins to phase out for that manufacturer.

Currently, no manufacturers have been phased out yet. To claim the credit, fill out IRS Form 8936, Qualified Plug-in Electric Drive Motor Vehicle Credit. For vehicles acquired for personal use, report the credit from Form 8936 on the appropriate line of your Form 1040, U.S. Individual Income Tax Return. For vehicles purchased in 2010 or later, this credit can be used toward the alternative minimum tax (AMT). To learn more about the law, visit the IRS's Plug-in Electric Drive Vehicle Credit webpage[10].

CHAPTER NINE

The Future of EV

Figure 11: Concept Car Nissan IMX[15]

As urbanisation increases – an additional 2.5 billion people will live in cities by 2050 – cities and suburbs will undergo significant transformations to create sustainable living conditions for their residents.

Energy and mobility are the twin pillars of these transformations and both will re□uire radical adaptation to meet the demographic and economic growth without increasing congestion

[15] https://www.nissan.co.uk/experience-nissan/concept-cars/nissan-imx.html

and pollution. The question is whether policymakers and business leaders can harness and combine them in ways that maximize their benefits for cost efficiency, economic growth and environment footprint. The Fourth Industrial Revolution offers an unprecedented opportunity. Figure 11 shows Concept Car Nissan IMX and this is a future concept.

Another scenario is called "EV30@30". This scenario is based on the assumption that governments will announce and implement new policies that will increase global EV (Figure 12) penetration to 30 percent of new car sales by 2030—a 30 percent sales share. This 30 percent share is roughly what is needed to begin to meet emission-reduction commitments made in the lead-up to the 2015 Paris climate talks. Under this scenario, the number of EVs on the road could reach 228 million by 2030 (Electric Vehicle Initiative, 2019).

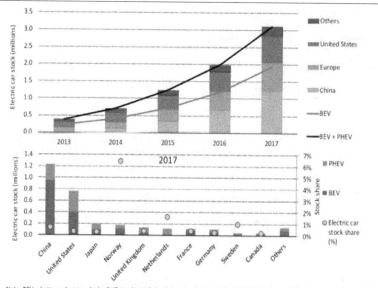

Note: BEV = battery electric vehicle; PHEV = plug-in hybrid electric vehicle. Stock shares are calculated based on country submissions and estimates of the rolling vehicle stocks developed for the IEA Mobility Model. The vehicle stocks are estimated based on new vehicle registration data, lifetime range of 13-18 years, and vehicle scrappage using a survival curve that declines linearly in the last five years of the active vehicle life. Lifetimes at the low end of the range are used for countries with higher income levels (and vice versa).

Source: IEA analysis based on country submissions, complemented ACEA (2018), EAFO (2018a).

Figure 12: EV Market Growth

EV Market Growth

In either case, whether there are 125 million EVs on the road in twelve years or 228 million, the result will be an impressive one, given that there were fewer than 1 million just four years ago.

Electric cars do represent an important transition technology; electrifying much of the global carfleet which can buy us the time we need to build zero-emission train and transit systems. Thus, it is very important that we move very rapidly to maximize the number of EVs built and sold. But the International Energy Agency (IEA) is clear: EV adoption will depend on ambitious, effective government action.

The 228 million EVs projected under the EV30@30 Scenario will only exist if governments implement a suite of aggressive new policies. The IEA states that:

"The uptake of electric vehicles is still largely driven by the policy environment. The ten leading countries in electric vehicle adoption all have a range of policies in place to promote the uptake of electric cars. Effective policy measures have proved instrumental in making electric vehicles more appealing to customers..., reducing risks for investors, and encouraging manufacturers to scale up production. Key examples of instruments employed by local and national governments to support EV deployment include public procurement programmes..., financial incentives to facilitate the acquisition of EVs and cut their usage cost (e.g. by offering free parking), and a variety of regulatory measures at different administrative levels, such as fuel-economy standards and restrictions on the circulation of vehicles based on tailpipe emissions performance" (Electric Vehicle Initiative, 2019).

Figure 13 shows the global EV stock in the new policy while figure 14 illustrates the EV Charging point.

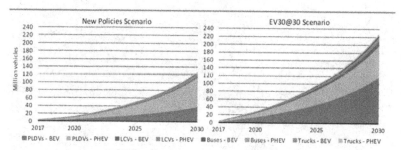

Notes: PLDVs = passenger light duty vehicles; LCVs = light commercial vehicles; BEVs = battery electric vehicles; PHEV = plug-in hybrid electric vehicles.

Source: IEA analysis developed with the IEA Mobility Model (IEA, 2018a).

Figure 13: Global EV Stock in the New Policies and EV30@30 Scenario 2017 – 2030

In 2018, about 95 million passenger cars and commercial vehicles were sold worldwide. About 1 million were electric— about 1 percent. The goal is to get to 30 percent in 12 years. Attaining that goal, and thereby averting some of the worst effects of climate change, will re☐uire Herculean efforts by policymakers, regulators, international bodies, and automakers.

Figure 14: Electric Car Charging Point

The number of electric vehicles on the road around the world will hit 125 million by 2030, the International Energy Agency forecasts.

- The world's fleet of electric vehicles grew 54 percent to about 3.1 million in 2017.

- The IEA says government policy will continue to be the linchpin for electric vehicle adoption.

These three steps will ensure the EV dominates the future:

1) **Take a multi-stakeholder and market-specific approach:** The investment and infrastructure required to support electric mobility will vary significantly from one place to another. Any roadmap to electric mobility should be adapted to three main characteristics of the specific market: local infrastructure and design; energy system; mobility culture and patterns. All relevant stakeholders should be engaged to collectively define a new paradigm for cities that go beyond today's industry divisions, in search of complementary municipal, regional and national policies.

2) **Prioritize high-use electric vehicles:** Electric taxis and public transportation will have a great impact on reducing carbon emissions. These types of vehicles are driven far more than personal-use vehicles, so commercial and public EV fleet development should be encouraged.

3) **Deploy critical charging infrastructure today while anticipating the mobility transformation:** EV charging infrastructure should be developed along highways, at destination points and close to public transportation nodes. This is critical for three reasons: first, to keep pace with current demand; second, to address a range of anxiety issues by making charging stations accessible, convenient and easy to locate; lastly, to promote the adoption of EVs in commercial and private markets (European Environmental Agency, 2018).

NIO - Chinese Electric Vehicle

After a first presentation in April 2017, NIO officially launched its ES8 electric SUV and with it full specs. The ES8's range as specified by the NEDC is at 355 kilometers provided by the model's 70 kW battery. It serves to power a 480 kW system that accelerates the seven-seater from 0 – 100 kph in 4.4 seconds and up to a top speed of 180 kph, according to NIO.

The NIO ES8 is a High-Performance Electric Flagship SUV[16] (figure 15). It is a mobile living space on wheels with performance in its DNA. Both the on-board NIO Pilot system, an advanced autonomous driving assistant system, and in-car intelligent AI system NOMI redefine the car ownership experience (Nio ES8, 2019). While NIO showcases their vision car; the autonomous car of the future (Figure 16 and 17).

High-Performance Electric Flagship SUV

Figure 15: NIO ES8 Electric SUV[16]

---

[16] https://www.nio.com/es8?noredirect=

NIO EVE: Vision Car Concept

Figure 16: Nio eve vision car concept: Vision of an autonomous car of the future[17]

Our vision for an autonomous car of the future.

Figure 17: Autonomous Car of the Future[17]

---

[17] https://www.nio.com/visioncar

EV Battery Swapping Stations

NIO also started a network of battery exchange stations, called Swap Stations and wants to install 1,100 across China by 2020. Investors appear to believe in NIO's vision as the latest round of financing (Motoward) resulted in an additional one billion dollars for the EV maker[12]. Figure 18 shows an example of EVs battery swapping station.

Figure 18: An Example of EVs Battery Swapping Station

In November 2016, the company unveiled its electric supercar, the NIO EP9, which achieved a new lap record at the Nürburgring Nordschliefe. On October 12, 2016, the EP9 lapped the 20.8km 'Green Hell' in 7m 05.12s, beating the previous EV lap record held, making it the fastest electric car in the world. Additionally, on November 4, 2016, it smashed the EV record at Circuit Paul Ricard in France, recording a time of 1m 52.78s, eclipsing the previous record of 2m 40s.

On February 23, 2017, the NIO EP9 drove autonomously without any interventions, recording a time of 2m 40.33s at a top speed of 160 miles per hour. The same day, the NIO EP9 also beat the fastest COTA lap time for a production car, achieving a lap time of 2m 11.30s and reaching a top speed of 170 miles per hour[18].

---

[18] https://www.nio.com/ep9

CHAPTER TEN

Advantages and Disadvantages of Electric Cars

The electric car (EV) is a relatively new concept in the world of the automobile industry. Although some companies have based their car models on the proactive use of electricity, some also offer hybrid vehicles that run on both electricity and gas. Electric cars such as the Nissan Leaf, Kia e-Niro, Jaguar I-Pace, Mercedes-Benz EQC, Hyundai Kona Electric the Ford Focus Electric, the Tesla Model S, and the Chevrolet Volt are a great way to save money, but also to help create a healthy and stable environment.

Internal combustion engine (ICE) cars produce a lot of carbon emissions that are released into the atmosphere, making us vulnerable to pollution and greenhouse gases. In order to contribute positively to the environment in which we live, an electric car is a big step forward. By buying an electric car, you can also receive government subsidies for your environmental conscience. Even though you may be paying more for your vehicle, the long-term positive aspects overshadow the drawbacks considerably.

Advantages of an electric car

An electric car is a great way for you, the consumer, to save a lot of money on gasoline. Moreover, there are so many reasons why you should invest in a state-of-the-art electric car.

1.No gasoline is needed, and it is cheap to run: Electricity is much cheaper than gasoline in the long run so driving an electric car can save you a huge amount of money. Gasoline prices are unpredictable and have reached some very high peaks in the past decade. With electric cars, this cost can be avoided (an average American spends between $2,000 and $4,000 in gasoline a year). Although electricity is not free, an electric car is much cheaper to run. And in the UK, fossil fuels like petrol and diesel are expensive, with UK prices highest around £1.27p per litre for unleaded petrol and £1.33p per litre for diesel as of June 2019.

2. Savings: Electric cars are inexpensive to recharge and hybrid models use less gas than conventional combustion engines. Both options are a great way to go green and save money. If you purchase select models, you can even qualify for government incentives to save more money on your new car purchase.

3. No emissions: Electric cars are 100% ecological because they work with electric motors. They do not release toxic gas or exhaust into the environment because they run with a clean source of energy. They are even better than hybrid cars because gas hybrids produce emissions. You will contribute to a healthy and green climate.

4. Popularity: Electric vehicles are gaining popularity. With the increase in popularity, all new types of cars are on the market, offering you a multitude of choices for the future.

5. Safe driving: Electric cars are subject to the same fitness tests and procedures as other fuel-powered cars. In the event of an accident, the airbags can be expected to open and the electricity to be disconnected from the battery. This can prevent the driver and passengers from serious injury.

6. Cost-effective: Previously, an electric car would have been too expensive for many people. But with technological advances, costs and maintenance have decreased. Mass production of batteries and available tax incentives have further reduced the cost, making it much more economical.

7. Reduced maintenance: Electric cars run on electric motors, so it is not necessary to lubricate the engines. Other expensive engine repairs will be a thing of the past. As a result, the maintenance cost of these cars has decreased. You do not need to send it for repairs often, as you do for a normal combustion engine car.

8. Reduction of noise pollution: Electric cars considerably limit noise pollution because they are much quieter. Electric motors are capable of providing a smooth drive with higher acceleration over long distances.

9. Eco-friendly materials: There is also a trend towards more eco-friendly production and materials for EVs. The Ford Focus Electric is made up of recycled materials and the padding is made out of bio-based materials.

The Nissan Leaf's interior and bodywork are partly made out of green materials such as recycled water bottles, plastic bags, old car parts and even secondhand home appliances

Many electric car owners have been reported saving up to tens of thousands of dollars a year. Given that oil demand will only increase as stocks run out, an electric car will most likely be the normal mode of transportation in the coming years. Companies like Nissan and Tesla offer excellent electric models offering an exceptional number of benefits to those who decide to invest. You will not only save yourself, but your family, huge sums of money. The environmental impact of an electric car is also zero, which means that you reduce your carbon footprint and have a positive impact on the economy.

Disadvantages of an Electric Car

Although the evidence of the positives has become very clear, there are also some downsides that one needs to consider before deciding to make an electric car the next big investment. These reasons are:

1. **Recharge Points:** Electric charging stations are still in the development stages. Not many places you go to daily will have electric charging stations for your vehicle, meaning that if you are on a long trip and run out of a charge, you may have difficulty locating a charging station. There are lots of investments being made on smart charging infrastructures to reduce range anxiety.

2. **Short Driving Range and Speed:** Electric cars are limited by range and speed. Most of these cars have a range of about 50-100 miles and now between 200 – 300 miles and then need to be recharged again. You just cannot use them for too long journeys as of now, although it is expected to improve in the future.

3. **Longer Recharge Time:** While it takes a couple of minutes to fuel your gasoline powered car, an electric car takes about 4-6 hours to get fully charged. Therefore, you need dedicated power stations as the time needed to recharge them is quite long.

4. **Silence as a Disadvantage:** Silence can be a bit of a disadvantage as people are used to hearing noise if cars are coming from behind them. An electric car is however silent and can lead to accidents in some cases.

5. **Not Suitable for Cities Facing a Shortage of Power:** As electric cars need power to charge up, cities already facing acute power shortages are not suitable for electric cars. The consumption of more power would hamper a city's power needs.

6. **Government Initiatives Are Limited:** Some governments do not provide money-saving initiatives in order to encourage you to buy an electric car.

7. **Electric Cars Are Still Expensive:** Some models of electric cars are still very expensive depending on how new they are and the technology it took to develop them.

Doing a fair bit of research into different models, and maybe even hybrids will help you make an accurate decision moving forward. However, no matter how you look at it, an electric car can save the precious environment. Figure 19 shows the cost of EVs in the market right now.

Current EVs (available now)

RANGE: **miles** | km
REGION ⓘ: **ALL** | US | EU
COMPARE: Range vs Price | Range vs Battery | Price per mile | Efficiency

Model		Price	Range (miles)	Battery (kWh)
BMW i3	EU US	$44,450	114	33
CHEVROLET Bolt EV	US	$36,620	238	60
FIAT 500e	US	$32,995	84	24
FORD Focus Electric	EU US	$29,120	115	33.5
HONDA Clarity Electric	US	$37,510	89	25.5
HYUNDAI Ioniq Electric	EU US	$29,500	124	28
HYUNDAI Kona Electric	EU US	$36,450	258	64
JAGUAR I-PACE	EU US	$76,500	234	90
KIA Soul EV	EU US	$33,950	111	30
NISSAN Leaf (1st Gen)	EU US	$30,680	107	30
NISSAN Leaf (2nd Gen)	EU US	$29,990	151	40
RENAULT Zoe	EU	$31,000	186	41
SMART ED	EU US	$23,800	100	17.6
TESLA Model 3 (Long Range)	EU US	$53,000	310	74
TESLA Model 3 (Mid Range)	US	$46,000	260	62
TESLA Model S 100D	EU US	$94,000	335	100
TESLA Model S 75D	EU US	$74,500	259	75
TESLA Model S P100D	EU US	$135,000	315	100
TESLA Model X 100D	EU US	$96,000	295	100
TESLA Model X 75D	EU US	$79,500	237	75
TESLA Model X P100D	EU US	$140,000	289	100
VOLKSWAGEN e-Golf	EU US	$30,495	119	35.8
VOLKSWAGEN e-Up!	EU	$34,500	99	18.7

EVs by Make

Number of full electric models (current and upcoming).

Audi
BMW
Chevrolet
Faraday Future
Fiat
Ford
Honda
Hyundai
Jaguar
Jeep
Kia
Lucid
Mazda
Mercedes-Benz
Mini
Mitsubishi
Nissan
Peugeot
Porsche
Renault
Rivian
Seat
Skoda
Smart
Subaru
Tesla
Toyota
Volkswagen
Volvo

Compare All

Prices shown in USD (or USD equivalent). This is the base price (MSRP), excluding any potential tax credits. Average new car price is $35285 (source).

Prices shown in USD (or USD equivalent). This is the base price (MSRP), excluding any potential tax credits. Average new car price[19] is $36590.

Figure 19: Current EV Available and Costs

[19] https://evrater.com/evs

Cost of Charging an Electric Car in the UK

A complete guide on how much it costs to charge an electric car in the UK at home, work and on the go as provided by PodPoint[20]:

Summary

The cost to charge an electric car in the UK varies between home, work and public charging. For a typical electric car with a 60kWh battery and 200-mile range:

Charging at home: Costs about £7.80 for a full charge.

Charging at work: Many employers will install workplace charging points and typically offer free access throughout the day.

Charging at public locations: Public charge points at supermarkets or car parks are often free to use for the duration of your stay.

Rapid charging: Rapid charging points are normally found at motorway service stations and typically cost £6.50 for a 30 min, 100-mile charge.

Cost to charge an electric car at home

Charging an electric car at home costs about £7.80 for a full charge and is the most convenient and cost-effective way to keep your car fully charged. Most drivers will charge their electric car overnight, waking up to a full battery every morning. Average domestic electricity rate is about 14p per kWh.

---

[20] https://pod-point.com/guides/driver/cost-of-charging-electric-car

Fully charging a 60kWh electric car will cost about £7.80 and give you about 200 miles of range. Find out more about the home charging options available and how fast they charge your car.

Tip: Charging at home is best done through a dedicated home chargepoint, which comes with a one-off cost starting at £279 with the government OLEV grant.

Cost to charge three popular electric cars:

Electric Cars	Battery size	Approximate "real-world" electric range	Cost to fully charge	Cost per mile
Nissan LEAF (2018)	40 kWh	150	£5.17	3.4p
Tesla Model S 100D	100 kWh	320	£12.93	4.0p
Mitsubishi Outlander PHEV (2019)	13.8 kWh	23	£1.78	7.8p (electric mode)

Cost to charge an electric car at work

The cost of charging an electric car at work can vary between organisations with some choosing to provide free charging while others set a paid tariff. Some employers offer free charging as a staff incentive. Others opt for a time-based tariff to encourage sharing of charging stations.

Another model is to offer free employee charging for a set period of time and then a fee for longer to encourage employees to vacate charging spaces.

Tip: More and more businesses around the UK are installing electric car charging facilities. Employee demand is one of the key drivers along with the sustainability benefits and reduced fleet costs.

Cost to charge an electric car at public charge points

Charging your electric car while out and about is a great way to top up your battery, and many locations offer free charging to their customers or visitors.

On most modern networks you can use a free-to-download mobile app to find charge points and start your charge.

Some older public charge points require an RFID card (similar to a contactless debit card) to start charging which can be ordered online.

For app-enabled charge points, if the host has set a tariff, you will be able to pay for your charge in the app.

Tip: Use a mapping service like the Pod Point App or Zap Map to find places to charge and remember to check which authentication method the chargepoint network uses before you travel

Cost to charge an electric car at rapid chargers

Rapid chargers are typically found in motorway service stations and range from being free to one of the more expensive ways to charge.

Pod Point's rapid chargers at Lidl are free to use, while Pod Point's Tesco units cost about £6.25 for 30 minutes of charging (about 100 miles of range).

The Tesla Supercharger Network has points across the UK which are often free to use for owners of Tesla electric vehicles.

Other sites can be found around the UK and typically have an associated tariff according to PodPoint[15].

CHAPTER ELEVEN

The Future of Electric Vehicles

While electric vehicles still account for a very small percentage of global car sales, auto companies have made significant investments in them. As governments move forward to raise emissions standards, even traditional manufacturers anticipate that electric vehicles will play an important role in the near future.

To this end, auto companies are planning to roll out super cool electric cars in the near future.

Here are some super cars that you will see on the road.

1. Porsche Taycan

Porsche stunned the world two years ago with the debut of its all-electric Mission E sedan concept, later promising it will go into production as the Taycan in 2020 (Road and Track).

Porsche Taycan

Porsche has said the Taycan will have a range of over 300 miles per charge, over 600 horsepower, and the ability to accelerate from 0-60 mph in less than 3.5 seconds (Perkins et al., 2019).

2. Volkswagen I.D. Buzz

Volkswagen is revamping its iconic minibus with the I.D. Buzz, which will reach dealerships in 2022 (Business Insider Australia[21])

.

Volkswagen I.D. Buzz[22]

The van will have a customisable interior.

---

[21] https://www.businessinsider.com.au/vw-microbus-launching-in-2022-will-have-big-updates-2018-1

Interior of Volkswagen I.D. Buzz[22]

It will feature seats that can move and rotate on tracks in the floor, allowing owners to set up the interior for a variety of purposes (Volkswagen, 2018).

---

[22] https://www.businessinsider.com/electric-cars-that-will-be-available-by-2025-2018-1?r=US&IR=T

3. Volkswagen I.D.

Volkswagen plans to release an Electric Compact Car, the I.D., In 2020. Volkswagen explained that the I.D. will have a range of up to 373 Miles.

Volkswagen I.D

Volkswagen has said the I.D. will have 168 horsepower.

The ID will be in the same price range as a Golf with similar specs and features. The Golf currently starts at a little over $20,000 - Driving Electric (Matousek, 2018).

4. Jaguar I-Pace

Jaguar released its first fully electric vehicle, the I-Pace, earlier this year. Jaguar says the I-Pace has the kind of performance specifications you would expect from a luxury brand.

Jaguar I-Pace[23]

---

[23] https://www.carscoops.com/2017/09/jaguar-i-pace-platform-could-spawn-new/

Interior of Jaguar I-Pace[24]

Designed as a competitor to Tesla's Model X, the I-Pace will have 394 horsepower, 512 pound-feet of torque, up to 292 miles of range and the ability to accelerate from 0-60 mph in 4.5 seconds, according to Jaguar[25].

---

[25]   https://www.jaguar.in/about-jaguar/concept-cars/i-pace-concept/index.html

5. Kia E-Niro

The new Kia e-Niro models equipped with long-distance 64 kWh battery packs are paired with a 150 kW (204 ps) motor, producing 395 Nm torque, enabling the e-Niro to accelerate from 0-to-100 kph in just 7.8 seconds. The standard 39.2 kWh battery pack is matched to a 100 kW (136 ps) motor, also producing 395 Nm torque, and accelerating to 100 kph from a standstill in 9.8 seconds and has a range between 282 miles to 301 miles. Like the Niro Hybrid and Plug-in Hybrid variants, the e-Niro is front-wheel drive.

Kia e-Niro Media[26]

[26]https://www.businessinsider.com/electric-cars-that-will-be-available-by-2025-2018-1?r=US&IR=T

Zero-emissions crossover combines electric power with crossover space and practicality, innovative technologies to harvest and conserve electric energy.

The e-Niro provides owners with a range of technologies to enhance battery efficiency and improve the car's range, including regenerative braking, Coasting Guide Control (CGC), and Predictive Energy Control (PEC). The technologies enable drivers to recharge the battery pack and maximise vehicle range when coasting or braking. CGC and PEC are linked to the navigation system and account for handling corners and topographic changes, suggesting when drivers could coast in order to harvest additional energy.

The e-Niro will be covered by Kia's industry-leading 7-Year, 150,000-kilometre warranty as standard. The warranty also covers the battery pack and electric motor (Alexiev, 2018).

6. Aston Martin Rapid E

Aston Martin will make only 155 Rapide E sedans, which will be sold in 2019. Aston Martin says the car will outdo Tesla. In September 2018, Aston Martin tested its first battery-electric sports car, the Rapide E. They stated that the Rapide E will be powered by an 800-volt battery system with 65kWh capacity, using over 5,600 lithium-ion 18650 format cylindrical cells. It will have a range of "over 200 miles" with a charging rate of 185 miles per hour using a typical 400V 50kW charger.

Aston Martin Rapid E[27]

The luxury car will cost $255,000, and Aston Martin's CEO says it will be superior to any of Tesla's offerings (Aston Martin, 2019).

---

[27] https://www.businessinsider.com/electric-cars-that-will-be-available-by-2025-2018-1?r=US&IR=T

7.Tesla Model Y

Tesla Model Y' is Tesla's upcoming crossover all-electric vehicle built on the same third generation platform as the Tesla Model 3. The vehicle is similar to the Model 3 and features similar options as the Model 3, like the Model S is similar to the Model X. Tesla unveiled the Model Y on March 15, 2019. It is expected to hit production in late 2020 (Lambert, 2019).

Tesla Model Y[28]

Musk said the Model Y will be a "manufacturing revolution."

---

[28] https://www.businessinsider.com/electric-cars-that-will-be-available-by-2025-2018-1?r=US&IR=T

During Tesla's first-quarter earnings call in May, 2019, Musk said the Model Y will transform Tesla's manufacturing process.

Tesla Model Y[29]

The Model Y will have up to 300 miles of range, according to Tesla. The Model Y will have between 230-300 miles of range, depending on the trim, Tesla says, as well as the ability to accelerate from 0-60 mph in as little as 3.5 seconds (Matousek, 2018).

[29] https://www.businessinsider.com/electric-cars-that-will-be-available-by-2025-2018-1?r=US&IR=T

8. Mercedes-Benz EQA

Mercedes-Benz has shown a concept for a compact electric car, called the EQA.

The EQA concept has a little less than 250 miles of range on road and track.

Mercedes-Benz EQA[30]

[30] https://www.businessinsider.com/electric-cars-that-will-be-available-by-2025-2018-1?r=US&IR=T

The concept has two motors, all-wheel-drive, and can accelerate from 0-60 mph in around 5 seconds. While Mercedes-Benz has not indicated when a production version of the EQA will arrive, the company has said it plans to invest $11 billion in electric vehicles by 2022, which suggests a production EQA could be on the horizon (Perkins, 2017).

9. Tesla Roadster

Tesla revealed its new Roadster in November 2017. The company said the car will be available in 2020.

Tesla Roadster[31]

---

[31] https://www.businessinsider.com/electric-cars-that-will-be-available-by-2025-2018-1?r=US&IR=T

The car will be incredibly fast, Tesla says. Tesla said the base version of the vehicle will be able to accelerate from 0-60 mph in 1.9 seconds, reach a top speed of 250 mph, and drive 620 miles per charge. Elon Musk said a premium version with a SpaceX upgrade package will include around 10 small rocket thrusters that will improve the vehicle's acceleration, maximum speed, braking, and handling (Matousek, 2018).

10.Nissan IDS

Nissan IDS[32]

[32] https://www.businessinsider.com/electric-cars-that-will-be-available-by-2025-2018-1?r=US&IR=T

Nissan hopes to have the self-driving technology for its electric, autonomous IDS ready by 2020, which means we could see the IDS by 2025 (Matousek, 2018).

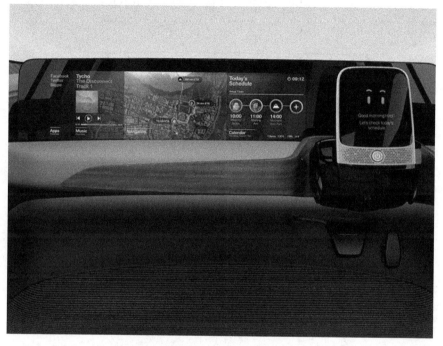

Interior of Nissan IDS[33]

The IDS will have a steering wheel that turns into a tablet.

Drivers will have the option to drive the car manually or have it drive autonomously. In its autonomous driving mode, the steering wheel folds into the dashboard and is replaced by a tablet that can be used to control an enormous touchscreen.

---

[33] https://www.businessinsider.com/electric-cars-that-will-be-available-by-2025-2018-1?r=US&IR=T

CHAPTER TWELVE

Social Impact of the Electric Vehicle

Electric cars will be the next revolutionary force in the transport and technology sector. They have the potential to change the way energy is used, created and redirected.

Electric cars are a solution to the deleterious environmental impact of conventional cars. Moreover, they have also proven to have many more benefits to society.

The advent of electric cars calls for an improvement in overall energy consumption and production. They have shown how important it is to find alternative sources of energy, and this can have a positive impact on the environment and society as a whole.

Social Impact of the Electric Vehicle

Better energy efficiency

Electric vehicles (EVs) are 75% efficient in converting input energy into motion energy (kinetic energy). On the other hand, gasoline vehicles equipped with an internal combustion engine (ICE) have an efficiency of 25%.

Electric cars, having fewer parts to channel energy, undergo less energy conversion. This results in less energy loss compared to gasoline engines. Even though electric car brakes do not work the same way as petrol car brakes: they have regenerative braking. This allows the car to charge the battery when braking!

Here's how this regenerative braking works:

Instead of using a brake pad that converts friction into heat, electric cars run on a generator that recovers some of the energy lost in the battery.

Less greenhouse emissions

One of the main reasons for introducing electric cars to the market is the concern over greenhouse gas emissions and their contribution to global warming.

The creation of electric cars to reduce or eliminate exhaust emissions is designed to combat this. Reducing carbon emissions has the biggest impact on urban areas, where millions of people drive cars.

The reduction of air pollution due to the elimination of exhaust pipes in electric cars promotes sustainable mobility. This greatly reduces the negative impact of transport needs on the atmosphere.

In addition, even if all the electricity from an electric car is produced from fossil fuels, it will still be less polluting than a gasoline car.

As we have already mentioned, electric cars are much more efficient than internal combustion engine (ICE) cars. This means that electric cars need less energy to operate than traditional gasoline cars.

Better for the environment

Overall, electric cars are significantly cleaner and safer for the environment than traditional gasoline cars.

Electric cars do not require drilling for oil (for fuel). In addition, they do not release exhaust and they are also very quiet.

The biggest risk to the environment for gasoline cars is air pollution and depletion of the ozone layer due to chemicals released...not to mention the oil and radiator chemicals that sometimes leak. These chemicals seep into the soil and water supply, causing damage to plants, wildlife and ultimately humans.

The metal parts of electric cars are not completely environmentally friendly and must be disposed of in a responsible manner, but they do not cause any damage to the environment during the car's use.

Parts unique to electric cars, such as lead and lithium batteries, do not promote smog, air pollution or water contamination during use. As they are disposed of responsibly, the global impact of car batteries and electric cars will have a positive impact on the environment.

Can potentially improve public health

The widespread introduction of electric cars could improve public health.

Exhaust emissions are one of the main negative impacts of internal combustion engines. Not only are they noxious, but they are filled with harmful gases.

Millions of cars in the last century have contributed to air pollution and a deterioration of quality of life of many people.

On the other hand, electric cars do not emit harmful gas and therefore do not contribute to the presence of gaseous chemicals in the air. With less air pollution from cars, air quality has a chance to improve, leading to improved health.

Exhaust pollutants cause health complications, such as asthma and bronchitis. Chemicals, such as carbon monoxide and benzene, prevent oxygen from entering the vital organs of the body and are linked to certain cancers.

Creates economic growth

The innovation and technology of the electric car contribute to economic growth.

The electricity generated to power cars and electric homes must come from somewhere. Often it comes from oil or coal, but it can come from solar, wind, hydro, nuclear or biofuel sources.

The growing demand for a constant and reliable power source for electric cars is enabling the growth of renewable energy sources, such as solar and wind.

While oil prices fluctuate considerably, the price of solar energy and other renewable energy sources remain relatively constant. In addition, there will never be a shortage of solar energy, unlike the oil shortage in the world.

This means that electric vehicle charging stations are more likely to buy electricity from renewable sources that are consistent and reliable. This is already true with many charging networks for electric vehicles, such as the Tesla Supercharger network.

Reducing fossil fuel emissions through the use of electric vehicles will also help prevent the economic damage caused by climate change.

Climate change is causing a lot of damage to the global economy. For example, rising temperatures are at the root of many natural disasters, such as droughts and hurricanes, which cause considerable damage.

Electric cars not only fuel economic growth but also reduce the damage caused by a harsh climate to the economy.

Electric vehicles are becoming more and more affordable

While electric cars have a higher initial cost than petrol cars, they are generally more affordable in the long run. Based on the total cost of ownership, electric vehicles with similar characteristics to gasoline cars are much more affordable (for most people).

In addition, electric cars are becoming cheaper and battery manufacturing prices are also falling. This means that electric vehicles will become even more affordable in the future.

The maintenance of an electric vehicle costs much less than a conventional gasoline vehicle.

Since electric cars simply run on batteries and electric motors, very few mechanical parts can break. This means less replacement costs in the future.

Moreover, as electric vehicles do not have engines, they don't require the engine maintenance that combustion engine cars do, for example it is not necessary to change the filter and the oil regularly.

Overall, electric cars are significantly easier to own and maintain than traditional cars. This convenience can cancel the higher purchase price of an electric vehicle for budget-conscious buyers.

Electricity and fuel costs in the US

Refueling electric cars is much cheaper than gasoline cars. Let's compare fuel costs, assuming electricity costs $0.11 per kilowatt-hour (kWh) and gas costs $3 per gallon.

An electric car like the base model Tesla Model 3 (which costs $35,000 before premiums) has a nominal range of 220 km in compliance with the EPA standard. With a battery of 50 kWh, this EV would cost only about $5.50 for a full charge.

On the other hand, a gasoline car like the Toyota Corolla has a fuel economy of 31 mpg. That means it would cost about $21 worth of fuel to travel the same 220 km in this internal combustion engine (ICE) car.

Overall, an average driver could save about $860 per year in gas costs when switching to an electric car. Some people can save even more!

The more you drive in an electric vehicle, the more you save on fuel compared to a gasoline car. In the long run, this helps offset the slightly higher cost of buying an EV.

Technological growth

The growing demand for electric cars has encouraged car manufacturers to make them better. It encourages innovation and economic growth.

To make electric cars accessible to more citizens, they must be more affordable while maintaining exceptional operation. This can only be achieved by improving the technology and materials used to make these cars. Having more clean energy technologies available allows this energy to be considered for other vehicles, such as ships and jets.

Electric cars have introduced a future in which green technologies are widely used and demanded. Because electric cars are not yet perfect, consumers will continue to demand improvements and lower costs. In turn, the car and energy engineers will be motivated to move forward with the technology until the electric cars really make the positive environmental impacts they were promised. New challenges and questions, such as knowing what to do with old electric car batteries, only fuel more discoveries and learning and therefore more solutions.

The battery, the main component of electric cars, is a major concern of critics because it has a limited life. Batteries are also toxic if they are disposed of incorrectly.

Because electric cars have been created not only to be economical but also environmentally friendly, scientists and engineers are invited to find solutions to the problem of the battery.

Whether this solution is effective recycling, or the creation of new types of batteries, the existence of electric cars drives progress and leads to the improvement in air quality.

CHAPTER THIRTEEN
Circular Economy

What Is a Circular Economy?

Circular economy is an economic system that is focused on managing resources, minimizing waste and making best use of resources. It is a process that should be implemented at the manufacturing stages to aim at regeneration of products that can last long (long life), can be repaired, reused, recycled, recovered and remanufactured. However, circular economy for EVs, should be aimed at regenerative manufacturing of electric cars by design that could retain as much value as possible, and will entail re-use, remanufacturing and recycling of components and materials of electric vehicles for applications in the automotive industry as well as in other manufacturing industries. Figure 18 illustrates the circular economy of EVs, while figure 19 demonstrates details of the vehicle life cycle.

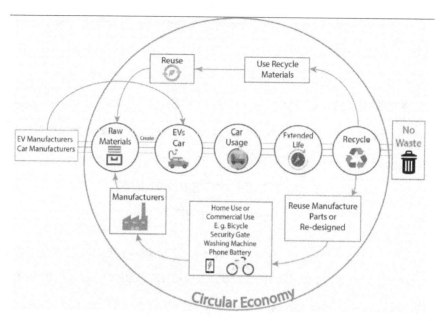

Figure 18: Circular Economy of EVs

Nowadays, driving an electric car is no longer a case of choosing between internal combustion engine (ICE) vehicles; petrol or diesel, but rather it exemplifies the future of transportation. It is not just a future technology revolution, but also a significant cultural shift and this will bring about changes in people's choices and perspectives with regards to the electric vehicles. Some of the drawbacks why EVs have not become popular with many people are:

- **The purchase cost:** Some EVs seem to be more expensive than a normal internal combustion engine vehicle. Although with government's incentives, and as mass
-

- production becomes available in the market, they will become cheaper to buy.

- **The EVs Charging Infrastructures:** If the infrastructure network and charging stations are efficient and widespread to all parts of the country in order to overcome, "Range Anxiety" – the fear of running out of battery electric power while driving or during mid-journey will be lessened.

The lack of enough widespread existing charging infrastructure is one of the greatest barriers to EVs market growth. The report by House of Commons (House of Commons HC 383, 2018) explained:

> The existing charging network is lacking both in size and geographic coverage, with the fastest ('rapid') charge points being particularly scarce. Analyses by the Energy Saving Trust and HSBC indicate that there are substantial disparities in the provision of public charge points across the country, with wide regional variations in both the average distance to a public charge point, and the ratio of public charge points to people. Such challenges are not unique to the UK: the need to improve charging infrastructure has been identified as one of the most significant barriers to EV development globally.

A visible and wide-reaching public charging network is essential to mitigate 'range anxiety' amongst would-be EV motorists:

- It will need to cater to the various travel needs of individual and commercial motorists, as well as to motorists with different levels of access to private charging facilities.

- Most EV users charge their vehicle at home overnight, and are expected to continue doing so, although workplace charging could also play an important role.

- Public charge points will be required in residential areas for the 40–50% of homes in the UK that do not have off-street parking, as well as at destinations such as town centres and retail parks, and at service stations to allow the completion of longer journeys. Destination and en-route charge points will need to be 'rapid' (taking 30 minutes to charge) or 'fast' (3–4 hours) to be useful and convenient.

- Charging infrastructure must also be readily accessible to motorists. The existing proliferation of multiple types of plugs and sockets, open access and subscription networks, payment systems and pricing regimes has meant that it has not always been easy for motorists to locate available charge points, to compare charge speeds and costs, and to equip themselves to pay for charging services across the country.

But this is changing now as countries across the world are investing in electric vehicle charging infrastructures. In Europe, the e-Mobility Revolution launched the National Plan for the installation of a charging infrastructure for electric vehicles and planned to set up over 28,000 charging points for 22kw charging, 50kw fast charging and up to 350kw Ultra-fast charging by 2022.

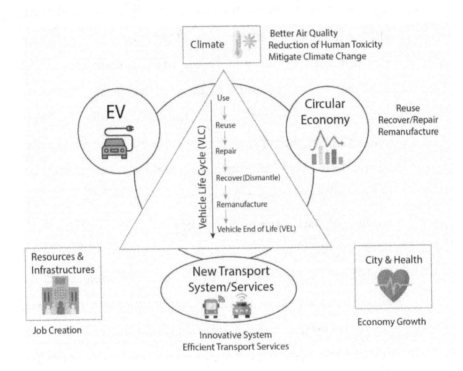

Figure 19: Vehicle Life Cycle (VLC)

The lifecycle analysis of EVs shows that since the target is to use renewable energy sources to charge the EVs, they emit zero CO_2 and zero greenhouse gas (GHG) in comparison with the conventional diesel vehicle. All these, in turn, will reduce air pollution, improve air quality, mitigate climate change and enhance economic growth. Likewise, as the technological improvement of EV battery increases, the reuse of battery for storage purposes, and the development of a recycling industry for EV batteries will lead to improvements in their sustainability.

Furthermore, the European Environmental Agency (TERM 2018) report expounded further on circular economy approaches (European Environmental Agency, 2018):

A circular economy approach presents opportunities to influence the future trajectories of these key variables by offering incentives for improvement, which will increase the benefits and reduce the negative impacts of battery electric vehicles (BEVs). For vehicle design, the most important component determining environmental impact is the battery. Here, standardisation of battery design could play a key role in helping ensure future battery reuse and recycling. Complementing this are designs that allow reduced inputs of raw materials alongside using alternatives at the very start of the process. Consumer expectations with regard to vehicle range will be key to future battery development. Larger (heavier) batteries provide greater energy storage and in turn vehicle range, and typically this increased vehicle range helps address consumer anxiety around using BEVs.

However, larger batteries require a greater quantity of raw materials and energy to produce, resulting in greater environmental impacts across all categories (UBA-DE, 2016), and the extra weight also leads to higher in-use energy requirement per kilometre. Impacts across the life cycle will be minimised if the automotive industry is incentivised to provide vehicles with modest ranges with ever-smaller batteries, as opposed to ever increasing ranges and associated increasing battery size. The density of the charging network and the time it takes to charge a BEV are also important factors affecting consumers' range expectations. To maximise vehicle range there is also an emphasis on the use of lighter materials in the vehicles, e.g. carbon composites. This can reduce use-stage energy consumption, but it can come at the cost of higher impacts during the production phase and lower recyclability of materials (Egede, 2017). In terms of overall impacts, when there is a trade-off between impacts in the use stage and those in other stages, the lifetime mileage of the BEV then becomes important. The higher the lifetime mileage of a vehicle, the lower the influence of production-related impacts. Lifetime mileage is itself, in part, a question of vehicle design. Lifetime mileage will be maximised if durability and ease of maintenance are prioritised in the design of individual components (especially the battery) and throughout the vehicle as a whole.

For vehicle use, the research highlighted that robust evidence on annual mileage, trip purpose and lifetime mileage is currently limited because consumer uptake of BEVs was very low until relatively recently.

Second, shared mobility, especially where it allows consumers access to a range of vehicles, could help ensure the choice of the most appropriate car for their needs. Third, while BEVs have an important role to play in terms of future mobility, it is essential to consider the role of BEVs alongside public transport and active travel (i.e. walking and cycling) modes. Reuse and recycling need to be 'designed in' to vehicles from the start. New processes need to be considered in the context of future access to rare earth elements (REEs) and steps taken to fully understand the barriers and opportunities for second-life applications and remanufacturing of batteries. There is a need to better understand the use of carbon composites and future recycling needs. The role of low-carbon electricity sources is important across all life-cycle stages to facilitate achieving the full GHG reduction potential from the use of BEVs. While this has the greatest impact in the in-use stage, it also relates to the raw material extraction and production stages, which involve energy-intensive processes. A reduction in the use of coal has further benefits in terms of reducing human ecotoxicity and the ecosystem impacts associated with coal mining and combustion. Related to this, the proportion of renewable generation sources in the electricity mix is expected to rise over the coming decades both in the EU (where BEVs are used) and in key cell and battery manufacturing locations outside the EU (Huo et al., 2015; EC, 2016)...).

CHAPTER FOURTEEN

Electric Vehicle VS. Gasoline Vehicles

Regardless of the type of vehicle you are looking to purchase, there are several costs associated with car ownership. Choosing an EV over a conventional, internal combustion engine (ICE) vehicle can result in significant long-term savings. If you are considering purchasing a new car and are also looking at an electric vehicle as a serious option, it is important to understand where your costs will come from, and how an electric vehicle can lead to different sources of spending and saving when compared to conventional ICEs.

Fuel Costs for Electric Cars vs. Gas-Powered Cars in the US

An immediately apparent difference between EVs and ICEs is their fuel source, and conse□uently what you as a consumer use to power your vehicle. ICEs run on gasoline burned internally to power the car, while EVs run on electricity. Electricity can come from many sources, including from the burning of coal or gas, or from renewable sources such as solar, wind, and hydropower.

A 2018 study from the University of Michigan's Transportation Research Institute found that electric vehicles cost less than half as much to operate as gas-powered cars. The average cost to operate an EV in the United States is $485 per year, while the average for a gasoline-powered vehicle is $1,117.

The exact price difference depends on gas and electric rates where you live, plus the type of car you drive. Depending on your vehicle's fuel efficiency rating, the money you spend to fill up your gas tank will translate to varying travel ranges. "Fuel-efficient" conventional cars are designed to maximize their miles per gallon (mpg) rating, thus costing the least amount of money per mile travelled. A car rated at 30 mpg will cost less money in fuel over time than a car rated at 20 mpg.

The cost to run an electric vehicle is slightly more complicated. Although you don't pay a gas pump-type fee every time you charge your EV battery, the electricity being used to charge your battery counts towards your home electric bill. You can directly compare electricity and gas costs when running an electric car vs. a conventional gas-powered car with the Department of Energy's eGallon[34] tool. This calculator is updated regularly, and compares the cost of driving a mile on gasoline vs. a mile on electricity, depending on where you live and energy prices at the time. Generally, the cost of electricity is decreasing in price, as renewable power generation costs fall lower and lower with advancements in technology and policy.

Fuel Cost Calculations for Electric Cars vs. ICE Cars in the UK

Nextgreencar provides a fuel cost calculator to compare the costs of two cars. You will be required to select vehicles using the drop-down lists, then enter mileage, frequency and MPG criteria and your results will appear. Based on your selections, the results will show cost per mile and weekly, monthly and annual fuel costs for both vehicles. The fuel cost calculator results are based on the current UK average petrol, diesel and electricity prices; these are editable if these do not reflect the prices you are paying in your area, or you wish to see the impact of a change in fuel prices according to Nextgreencar[35].

---

[34] https://www.energy.gov/maps/egallon

[35] https://www.nextgreencar.com/tools/fuel-cost-calculator/

Maintenance costs for EVs vs. Fossil Fuel Powered Cars

The fuel used to power your car is only one factor in the cost of car ownership. In particular, vehicle maintenance costs can stack up over time. With ICEs, engine maintenance can be a huge money sink, especially as cars age. Changing the engine oil, coolant, transmission fluid, and belts can add up over time. By comparison, electric cars don't have internal combustion engines, so these costs disappear. Universal vehicle expenses like tire and brake pad replacements, insurance, and structural repair are part of owning any vehicle, but EV owners avoid many of the repeated costs associated with combustion engine upkeep.

EVs are not without expense, however. The largest possible maintenance expense for an electric vehicle is a replacement battery pack. Unlike a conventional battery, EVs have large, complex rechargeable batteries that are drained and recharged constantly, which leads to degradation and range loss over time. In the rare case that your EV battery is defective and needs replacement, manufacturers will often cover that replacement with a battery warranty. However, if your car is not under warranty, replacing your EV battery is expensive. The vast majority of EV owners won't have to replace their car's battery, but it is a risk you run when operating an electric car.

Electric Car Rebates and Incentives

A great reason to go with an electric vehicle is of the current federal and state incentives available. These rebates help offset the typically higher cost of an electric car to make "going electric" more financially feasible. Rebates and incentives for EVs are changing constantly, and it's important to know what kinds of incentives are available near you. You can learn more about federal and state EV incentives in EnergySage's guide to electric car tax credits.

The availability of incentives for buying electric vehicles, coupled with their continuously falling costs, has made an investment in an EV a smart energy and money decision. Electric vehicles are not for every lifestyle, but when compared to the myriad costs surrounding ICE purchase and maintenance, choosing an EV can be an intelligent fiscal decision.

Sustainable Development of EV

Governments within the EU and the European Parliament have therefore realised the importance of sustainable development and have recently set goals like reducing greenhouse gas (GHG) emissions by at least 40% by 2030 and 80% by 2050.

To meet the emission targets[36], electric vehicles (EVs) are suggested to several organisations as a solution due to zero emissions when used in traffic, but there might be some implications that have to be accounted for in order to achieve a sustainable development of road transport.

---

[36] https://www.iea.org/media/topics/transport/3030CampaignDocumentFinal.pdf

CONCLUSION

In conclusion, the global impact of the electric vehicle revolution will benefit society. In the future (which is now), all cars will be electric. In fact, many car manufacturers have already committed to having a complete electric fleet in just a few decades. We are in a new era of transportation, where cleaner running cars (which are also affordable) are a reality.

Adopting this electric vehicle revolution will not only help solve our environmental problem but will also promote public health, economic growth, job creation, improve air quality, sustainable transportation system, mitigate climate change and fuel technological innovation, the pillar of society. It is time to embrace change and look to the future.

Now, the EV range anxiety is being solved by car manufacturers by designing long range EVs, providing energy stations that can recharge an EV battery within a short period of time, having accessible and availabilities of smart charging infrastructures across cities; car parks, on-street EV charging points, supermarkets EV Charging Points, public car park EV Charging points, and with EV home charging infrastructure. This will make EVs more attractive to buy and affordable to all.

REFERENCES

World Health Organization. (2019). WHO: *Ambient air pollution - a major threat to health and climate.* Retrieved from https://www.who.int/airpollution/ambient/en/

Roberts, M. (Health Editor). (2016 February 23). *UK air pollution 'linked to 40,000 early deaths a year'.* [BBC News Online]. London: BBC News. Retrieved from https://www.bbc.co.uk/news/health-35629034

House of Commons. House of Commons, Business, Energy, Industrial Strategy Committee. (2018). *Electric Vehicles: driving the transition* (HC 383). London: House of Commons. Retrieved from

https://publications.parliament.uk/pa/cm201719/cmselect /cmbeis/383/383.pdf

Hall, D., Moultak, M., Lutsey, N. (2017). *Electric Vehicle Capitals of The World Demonstrating The Path To Electric Drive.* The International Council on Clean Transportation (ICCT White Paper). Washington DC: ICCT. Retrieved from https://theicct.org/sites/default/files/publications/Global -EV-Capitals_White-Paper_06032017_vF.pdf

Alternative Fuels Data Centre. (2019). AFDC: *How Do All-Electric Cars Work.* Retrieved from https://afdc.energy.gov/vehicles/how-do-all-electric-cars-work

NIO ES8. (2019). *High-Performance Electric Flagship SUV.* Retrieved from https://www.nio.com/es8?noredirect=

NIO EVE VISION. (2019). NIO EVE our VISION CAR, showcases the future of autonomous driving. Retrieved from https://www.nio.com/visioncar

Electrive. (2019). *Nio completes first battery swapping route.* Retrieved from https://www.electrive.com/2019/01/20/nio-completes-first-battery-swapping-route/

PodPoint. (2019). *Cost of Charging Electric Car.* Retrieved from https://pod-point.com/guides/driver/cost-of-charging-electric-car

AA. (2018). *How to Find and Use EV Charge Points in Europe: Charging around Europe in an Electric Vehicle.* Retrieved from https://www.theaa.com/european-breakdown-cover/driving-in-europe/charging-around-europe-in-an-electric-vehicle.

Smith, L.J. (2019). *Solar power electric car charging stations coming to UK charges batteries in 10 minutes.* Retrieved from https://www.express.co.uk/life-style/cars/1145600/Solar-power-electric-car-charging-stations-UK-batteries-10-minutes

Schwierz , P. (2017). *VW in China, Nio, BYD, Citroën, MG.* Retrieved from https://www.electrive.com/2017/04/20/vw-in-china-nio-byd-citroen-mg/

Perkins, C. Petrany, M. (2019). *2020 Porsche Taycan: Here's What We Know: Porsche's first all-electric car should arrive next year. Here's what to expect.* Retrieved from https://www.roadandtrack.com/new-cars/future-cars/a12778510/2020-porsche-mission-e-news-photos-price-release/

Driving Electric. (2018). *Volkswagen ID. Buzz 2022: specs and on-sale date.* Retrieved from https://www.drivingelectric.com/volkswagen/784/volkswagen-id-buzz-2022-specs-and-sale-date

Jaguar. (2019). *I-PACE CONCEPT: Introducing I-PACE Concept, a preview of Jaguar's first all-electric five-seater sports car.* Retrieved from https://www.jaguar.in/about-jaguar/concept-cars/i-pace-concept/index.html

Aston Martin. (2019). *Rapide E: The First All-Electric Aston Martin.* Retrieved from https://www.astonmartin.com/en-gb/models/rapide-e

Perkins, C. (2017). *The Mercedes Concept EQA Is a 268-HP Electric Hot Hatch.* Retrieved from https://www.roadandtrack.com/car-shows/frankfurt-auto-show/a12226119/mercedes-concept-eqa/

Matousek, M. (2019). *40 electric cars you'll see on the road by 2025.* Retrieved from https://www.businessinsider.com/electric-cars-that-will-be-available-by-2025-2018-1?r=US&IR=T

European Environmental Agency. (2018). *Electric vehicles from life cycle and circular economy perspectives - TERM 2018: Transport and Environment Reporting Mechanism (TERM)*. (ISSN 1977-8449). Luxembourg: Publications Office of the European Union.

Boren, S., Ny, H. (2016). A Strategic Sustainability Analysis of Electric Vehicles in EU Today and Towards 2050, International Journal of Environmental and Ecological Engineering 10(3), 294-302

Alexiev, V. (2018). *The new Kia Niro EV: The e-Niro will be unveiled at 2018 Paris Motor Show: Press Release*. Retried from https://press.kia.com/eu/en/home/media-resouces/press-releases/2018/The_new_Kia_Niro_EV.html

Electric Vehicle Initiative. (2019). *Clean Energy Ministerial – Accelerating the transition to clean energy technologies: EV30@30 Campaign*. Retrieved from https://www.iea.org/media/topics/transport/3030CampaignDocumentFinal.pdf

Bawden, T. (2019). *Owners of electric vehicles could soon be able to charge their cars while driving*. Retrieved from https://inews.co.uk/news/science/electric-vehicles-charge-wireless-e-lanes-road-coventry/

EVSE. (2019). *Industry-leading EV Charging Manufacturer*. Retrieved from https://www.evse.com/

EVgo. (2019). *EVgo: Electric Vehicle (EV) Charging Stations: EV Fast Charging - Charge in Minutes, Not Hours.* Retrieved from https://www.evgo.com/

Nissan. (2019). *Nissan IMx - Experience Nissan: Concept Car Nissan IMX.* Retrieved from https://www.nissan.co.uk/experience-nissan/concept-cars/nissan-imx.html

Lambert, F. (2019). *Tesla confirms Model Y production progress at Fremont factory, on track for fall 2020 - Electrek.* Retrieved from https://electrek.co/2019/07/24/tesla-model-y-production-fremont-factory-fall-2020/

ABOUT THE AUTHOR

Dr. Taiwo Ayodele is a Lecturer, an Entrepreneur and an IT Consultant by profession. He is also an expert in Artificial Intelligence & Machine Learning, and Intelligent Systems. He is a consultant in Future Transportation and Sustainable Development (Advisor), as well as author of many books, academic journal articles and conference papers and proceedings.

CPSIA information can be obtained
at www.ICGtesting.com
Printed in the USA
LVHW051617040121
675669LV00050B/3445

9 781690 837107